SAINT-JULIEN

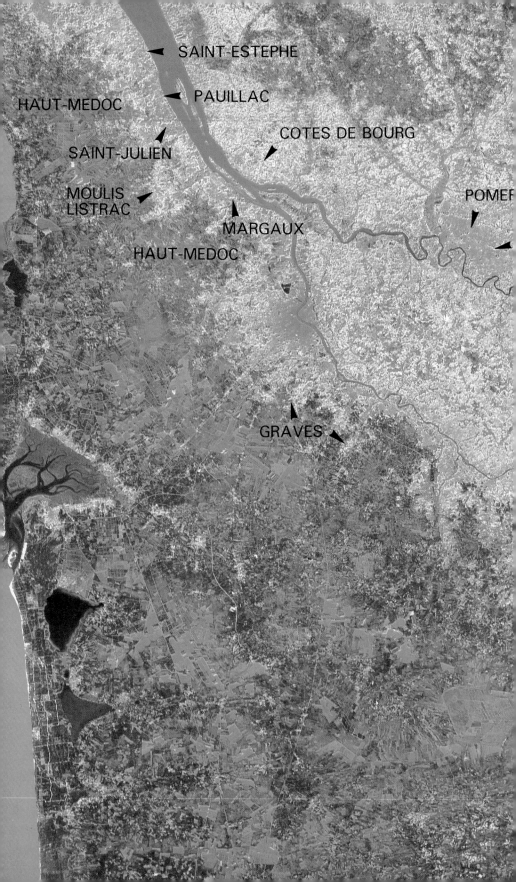

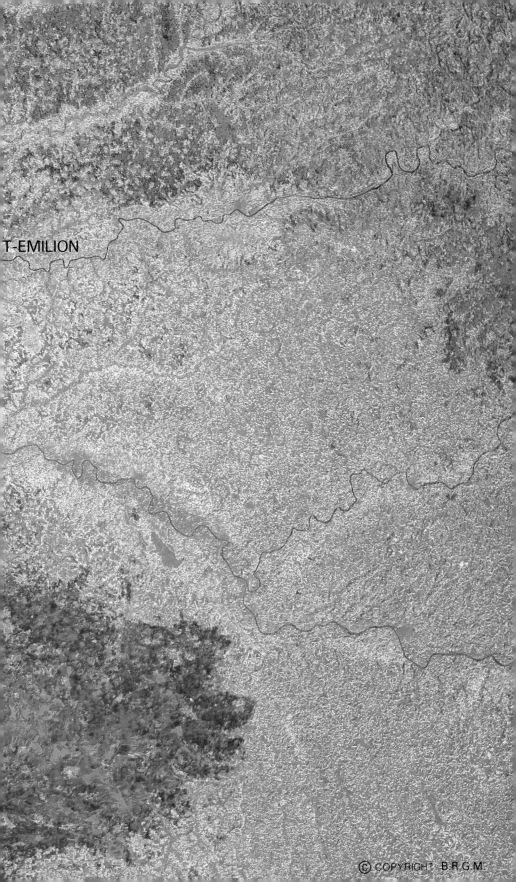

T-EMILION

The Saint-Julien appellation

Extent of the vineyard

AOC Haut Médoc

1 km

Based on the 1/50,000 map of the
I.G.N. Cartographie Graindorge, Paris

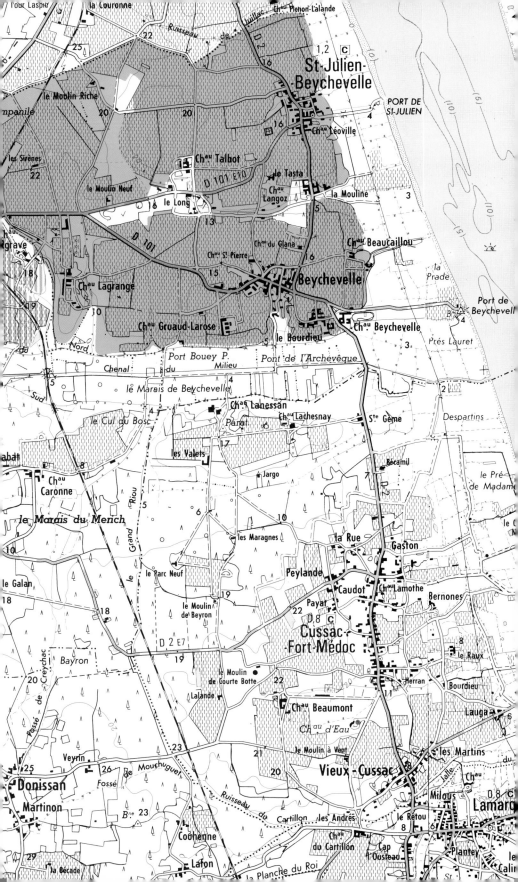

THE WINES OF FRANCE

SAINT-JULIEN

Bernard Ginestet

Foreword by Hugh Johnson

Holt, Rinehart and Winston
New York

First published in the United States in January 1986 by
Holt, Rinehart and Winston, 383 Madison Avenue,
New York, New York 10017.

Published simultaneously in Canada by Holt, Rinehart and
Winston of Canada, Limited.

Originally published in France under the title *Saint-Julien* by
Librairie Fernand Nathan.

Library of Congress Cataloging-in-Publication Data
Ginestet, Bernard.
   The wines of France.

   Translation of: Saint-Julien.
   1. Wine and wine making — France — Saint-Julien —
Beychevelle. I. Title.
TP553.G5813 1985   641.2'22'094471   85–17854
ISBN 0–03–006017–6

First American Edition

Designer: Henri Marganne

Printed in Holland

10 9 8 7 6 5 4 3 2 1

ISBN 0-03-006017-6

Contents

Measurements

1 hectare = 10,000 square metres = 2.471 acres
1 are = 100 square metres = 119.6 square yards

1 kilometre = 0.6214 mile (5/8 mile)
1 metre = 39.37 inches

1 *tonneau* = 9 hectolitres
1 hectolitre = 100 litres = 22 gallons (26.5 US gallons)
1 litre = 1.76 pints or 0.22 gallon (0.265 US gallon)

1 *journal* = 'the area of vines that can be worked by one
man in a day'

Foreword

The range and focus of the discussion of wine over the last ten years or so has been like a zoom lens dissolving a crowd scene to pick on a granule of the big picture. From the days when Lichine's *The Wines of France* was considered a pretty specialized book, publishers moved, not at all long ago, to regional volumes on Bordeaux, Burgundy and the other famous vineyards. With this series wine-scholarship takes the logical next step: it focuses on the commune as the unit, at the same time narrowing the focus and allowing us a far greater insight into its components, its methods and motives.

There is a more microscopic view still: that of the individual property. *Premiers crus* and other lordly estates with long histories are suitable subjects for such treatment, but not on the whole the wine-growing property of the middle to upper rank, whose historical peculiarities are less important than their present-day make-up and morale. For them it seems eminently appropriate to take the communal view: close enough to enjoy the detail, but distant enough to make useful comparisons.

This series differs in another, perhaps even more important way from the great majority of books about wine. Most authors review the subject from the standpoint of a more or less disinterested observer and consumer. This makes them strong on comparison – at any rate superficially – but often weak on insight. Bernard Ginestet is an author who addresses the world from the very heart of his theme. He is a passionately involved insider in Bordeaux, a man who has made a score of vintages, has dealt in the biggest stakes in the business as proprietor of Château Margaux, has participated in the manoeuvres of the market as a *négociant*. A man not to be fooled: enthusiastic, yes, but not starry-eyed. Steeped as he is in the region, he cannot hide his feelings for long. Sometimes they are written on the lines, sometimes between them. Always, even behind some seemingly bland report, you feel the beat of the author's pulse.

Facts and statistics are the bare bones of the books. No detail of *encépagement*, of vinification, of production or availability or soil; no label, no telephone number even is omitted. The flesh on these bones is history, anecdote, and above all experience.

The story starts with the physical and historical groundwork, including new geological maps in fascinating detail. The heart of the introduction is the gastronomic question – what is the identity of this appellation? How do you recognize its wines? How do its citizens view them, use them, and marry them with local ingredients in local dishes?

The repertoire of châteaux follows, leaving nothing out: a piece of research of inestimable value that goes far beyond any other document I know in its scope, even leaving aside the author's deep involvement with his subject. It does not attempt to be particular about wines and vintages. This is not a book of tasting notes – rather the book that enables you to taste with discrimination; to know what it is you are tasting and to draw accurate conclusions. The single consistent conclusion that the author draws is the *rapport qualité-prix*, or value-for-money, indicated by a row of glasses. The more full glasses, the higher his rating.

The photographs, specially commissioned for the series, do not need my encomiums. I need only say that each volume can teach you more about each parish than would a dozen visits without such a guide.

Hugh Johnson

*'Le vin fait que nos coeurs
sont des livres ouverts'*
Bailly, 1650

The Story of
the Saint-Julien Appellation

'Visitors – you are entering the ancient and celebrated region of Saint-Julien. Please pay your respects!' This is the way the local people welcome you as you travel along the D2 road from Bordeaux. You will have crossed the famous regions of Margaux, Lamarque and Cussac-Fort-Médoc and finally the meadows stretching below the hills of Beychevelle. A metal sign, painted in the style of a Gothic parchment, greets the visitor with instructions to salute the area. So, dear reader, before proceeding any further with your exciting discovery of this hallowed land, please pause for a moment and pay your respects.

◄A composition by Mme Henriette Moreau dedicated to the glory of Saint-Julien.

In France the art of the table is a religion; both cheese and wine have their patron saints. The most famous among the former are almost certainly Saint-Marcellin, Saint-Nectaire and Saint-Paulin. As for the latter they are certainly the Bordeaux trilogy of Saint-Emilion, Saint-Estèphe and Saint-Julien, the three Kings from the East dispensing their liquid treasure throughout the world, that 'intellectual gold' so highly praised by Baudelaire. The fame of Saint-Julien is particularly great in relation to its size.

The vineyard of Saint-Julien imparts to the visitor a feeling of superb calm. If we pause in the middle of the central plateau, with Lagrange to the west and the village of Beychevelle to the east, and with Talbot to the north and Gruaud-Larose to the south, we are overcome by a contemplative mood. The vine reigns supreme. Like a peaceful ocean with thousands of motionless waves, this triumph of cultivation makes us respect the creative genius of the men who made it. The low, twisted vine merges with the poor, stony soil in an alliance of vegetable and mineral forces, creating a superior order. Even before considering the final product of this process, and the mysterious alchemy so essential in the creation of a *grand cru*, we are seized with admiration. It is then that we can really understand the word 'vineyard'.

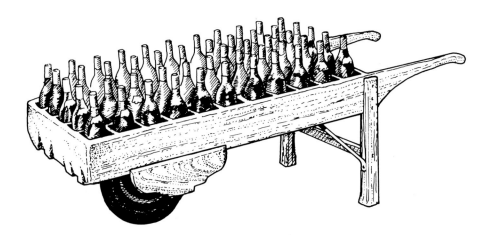

If it were necessary to give to the world an example of the noble French vineyard, Saint-Julien could be chosen as an archetype. An example of ten square metres would be sufficient to show the hypsometry, the hydrography and the surface geology of the appellation. It would include the essential Gironde estuary, the thick layers of stones, the complicated system of streams ensuring surface drainage, and the islets with their castles and *chais*, the parks and gardens

stretching out in straight lines. Professor Emile Peynaud, who is by temperament and training more technical than romantic, speaks of Saint-Julien in lyrical terms, as if this meeting place of chance and human necessity possessed the enchantment necessary to turn a scientist into a poet. A century ago, Professor Babrius declared that 'the history of wine is the history of the world.' He, too, was overcome by the eloquence which often characterizes the style of wine writers. There is, however, some truth in his words. The eternal themes of art are, for example, God, love, war, life and death. Throughout the ages wine has been linked with these, and its presence carries with it Dionysian influence, without which human passions would lose their colour, their zest and their vitality. . .

This aerial photograph shows the coastline of the Saint-Julien vineyard. In the foreground is the village of Saint-Julien; Beychevelle is at the top left.

The great highway of wine, that is, the Gironde, enters the Bordeaux region where it blends the mountain waters with those of the ocean. At this meeting point the pebbles, worn down by their long journey, are scattered along the low banks of the river. At Margaux most of the pebbles are from the Pyrenees. At Saint-Julien the stones come from the Garonne and the Dordogne. This mixture of pebbles, slowly broken down and smoothed through thousands of years, is unique. And the river is always at work, slowly producing its pebbly offspring.

The Pont de l'Archevêque crosses the Jalle du Nord, which marks the southern border of the Saint-Julien appellation. The bridge is named after the tradition during which the archbishop of Bordeaux would cross the bridge on foot to be greeted by the parishioners of Saint-Julien and Beychevelle.

All the conditions necessary to produce a major work of art are here, at Saint-Julien.

The appellation is remarkable in that it produces an extraordinarily constant level of quality. We could even go so far as to say that there are no 'small wines' at Saint-Julien. (Even in indifferent vintage years, the *crus* are still considered first-class.) Whether the châteaux are 'classified' or not is a contentious question, depending on the Bordeaux Chamber of Commerces' decision of 1855. In fact the average classification of Saint-Julien, *par équipes*, is the highest in the entire Médoc region.

In order to arrive at a precise figure, we need only to add the coefficients of the five categories of 1855 and divide them by the number of *crus* included in them. Saint-Julien is the first, with 300 points, followed by Margaux (290), Saint-Estèphe (280), Pauillac (193) and Haut-Médoc (160). This is one way of interpreting the statistics. It is not a decisive method but it can be considered significant in that it reveals the very high average level of Saint-Julien which does not include any *1e* or *5e crus*. At the time of the 1855 classification, the idea of an AOC wine did not exist. Each *cru* referred only to the relevant parish. The present assessment of AOC wines of the Médoc is unconnected with the wine-producing geographical area as it was known and understood in the mid-nineteenth century. One hundred years after the individual classification of the best *crus*, the best estates have now been classified on a collective basis. As with all such systems, these classifications must inevitably be eroded with the passage of time. Saint-Julien, however, with the microclimatic conditions existing at the châteaux and the unitary system of appellation, would appear to be very much an 'area' in the geographical sense of the word. Its characteristics are both simple and complex. Complex if we wish to consider separately each of its individual characteristics and simple if we consider it as a unit like an original molecule of a natural element. If we wish to place the AOC wines in a hierarchy comparable to those of the *grand crus* of the Médoc, Saint-Julien could claim to be in the first rank. I would support this argument.

The intention of the series in which this book is included is to give as detailed a list as possible of the AOC wines of Bordeaux. The description given for each wine-producing region will be as all-encompassing as possible. The list of the *crus* will be in the form of a dictionary. The relatively small number of representative labels from Saint-Julien (half as many as from Margaux) has allowed for more information in the introduction. As Saint-Julien is in the centre of the Haut-Médoc, the historical connection of the entire region can also be included. As an amateur film maker, I have tried to use a variable focus to connect the past history of this area, as it may have existed, with the various classic standard works of reference. The reader who is only interested in the present day could therefore easily pass over the second part of the introduction which follows. Without wishing to turn history upside down, I have nevertheless attempted to throw some light (albeit from a long distance) on to some of the lesser-known aspects of the history of Médoc and Bordeaux.

The best *escargots à la Bordelaise* of the entire Médoc region can be found at Henriette Moreau's restaurant, the Bar Restaurant du Square at Saint-Julien (Tel 59 08 26). The restaurant is modest in appearance. You can simply drop in, although it is wiser to telephone, not because you need to reserve a table but to give notice of your

arrival. Henriette Moreau both serves at table and works in the kitchen. Somehow she finds the time as well to chat with the guests and to describe her experiences that cover three generations and are enriched by family anecdotes. Her menu is not an encyclopedia of culinary art but her recipes are delicious. She deserves to be treated with courtesy and affection. A guest allergic to snails could well choose an eel soup and become a devotee for life, or he could try traditional regional cooking and choose the delicious sweetbreads prepared as our grandmothers did at the beginning of the century, and enjoy a few

The only restaurant in the area is to be found in the small main square of the village of Saint-Julien, near the town hall. It is owned by Mme Henriette Moreau.

glasses of wine and some *liqueur à la menthe*. If you are particularly favoured, between the cheese and the *gâteaux maison*, the *Médoc au chocolat*, she will show you her collection of photographs and articles on every aspect of Médoc life, ranging from turtle-dove shooting to the magnificent receptions given by the Rothschild family. An artist at heart, she is happy to leave her saucepans to take up her paint brushes or to write poetry. Her one problem is that she does not have enough time to achieve everything she would like to do. If you really wish to meet a true inhabitant of Médoc, make a point of visiting Henriette Moreau at Saint-Julien ... unless of course you happen to be lunching with the Borie family at Ducru-Beaucaillou or with Jean Cordier at Talbot. With these people, however, you need to do more than book in advance – you have to be invited.

I know from my own experience that it is not enough, in discussing wine, to give details of the yield per hectare, the length of fermentation, the level of glycerol or the advantages of the vintage. There is much more to say that is often almost impossible to express. I once

Fishing for eels is part of the local tradition; they are caught both on a line, and in special wickerwork baskets.

spent an entire afternoon looking at Picasso's *Guernica*, and when I left the Museum of Modern Art in New York my head was bursting with ideas without my being able to express a single word. It then occurred to me that I should write!

My father, Pierre Ginestet, who was the founder and Chancellor of the Académie du Vin de Bordeaux, once wrote: 'When you offer a Bordeaux wine that is worthy of this name, you should use the same reverent tone as you would in discussing a masterpiece or a symphony.' Such fatherly advice is much easier to give than to follow. If, however, the Latin humanism of my father does not encourage you to read this book, allow me to refer to Pliny and paraphrase him as follows: 'I shall speak of wine with the seriousness of a Médocian who is devoted to art and science. I shall speak of wine like a judge who is concerned with the health of humanity.'

Visitors, you are about to enter the ancient and famous vineyard of Saint-Julien. Please take the trouble to pay a visit.

I

In 1871 two boatmen, Vergnes and Petit, were working at the port of Saint-Julien and five others, the Andrivet brothers, Benoît, Larose and Andrivet Junior, worked at the port of Beychevelle. They were the owners of large, handsome barges carrying merchandise around the estuary, either following the coast between Lamarque and Saint-Estèphe, or crossing to Bourg, Blaye and Mortagne. They also sailed up the Garonne as far as Bordeaux and up the Dordogne as far as Libourne. That year they carried 2846 casks of wine to the commune of Saint-Julien and loaded 4207 casks there. The same year saw the beginning of a decline in river traffic as the newly built railway started to take over the business. The barge owners gradually disappeared and the two ports of Saint-Julien silted up.

These barges were large sailing vessels, well designed for local conditions, easy to load and unload and all built on the same design as the original *gabarit* imported from Holland as early as the fifteenth century. Up until the end of the nineteenth century they had almost a complete monopoly of trade on both banks of the river. They were also responsible for the transport of the white stone from La Roque de Thau, Bourg or Marcamps across the Gironde, where it was used to build the villages and castles of Médoc.

◄*Barges at the entrance to the port of Beychevelle, at the beginning of this century.* 27

Libourne — HENRY Guillier, rue Fonneuve

(9358) St-JULIEN-BEYCHEVELLE (Médoc).   Sur la Gironde.
PAQUEBOT DES MESSAGERIES MARITIMES EN PARTANCE POUR L'AMÉRIQUE.

Until the thirties a steamer offered a direct service from Saint-Julien-Beychevelle to the USA. The barges loaded the ship with large wine casks which contained all the major crus of the appellation. It was the end of an era.

Each of the four Médoc appellations (Margaux, Saint-Julien, Pauillac and Saint-Estèphe) had its own shipping service. Margaux is situated at the end of the course of the Garonne, hemmed in by a series of islands, while the other three give on to the estuary, further downstream from the Bec d'Ambes. With the construction of the railway and road networks, the riverside communes lost their business in the north. They were, until the beginning of this century, very dependent on the river and turned their backs on the interior. As you will see, all the façades of the châteaux were built below the stony slopes facing the river in contrast to those of the Côtes de Blaye and the Côtes de Bourg. Travelling along the D2 road towards Bordeaux-Pauillac, we cross the Saint-Julien vineyard. The châteaux to the right (Beychevelle, Ducru-Beaucaillou) can only be seen from behind. In order properly to understand the geographical nature of these parishes of the Haut-Médoc, we should travel along the left bank of the river. We now see them from a different perspective and can realize why and how these earlier communities were set up and organized. We see the church towers standing like familiar guards, acting as landmarks for sailors on the flat Médoc horizon. From time to time we also see a gracious façade, glimpsed through the green trees of a park and surrounded by *chais* and vines. We see the many narrow streams flowing from the interior and acting as borders between two communes or appellations. We see the cabins built on stilts where the local people come to fish with circular nets, and the many artificial pools next to half-buried cabins where the local wine-producers come to shoot wild duck in the early hours of the morning. We see the remains of the former landing places and their neighbouring buildings. We see the undulating stony hills with their superb vineyards like enormous counterpanes with a thousand stripes. Perhaps we will imagine we hear a Gascon voice from the past bidding us to lower the sail. Obeying the command we will lower the main sail and cross the current, our prow pointing to the west in order to make course for the entrance of the port of Beychevelle.

The Saint-Julien appellation is the smallest of the four glorious names of the Médoc. It covers about 805 hectares, of which 40 are covered with young plants which do not yet have the right to the AOC designation. On the southern border is a small river called the Jalle du Nord which is a continuation of the Jalle de l'Horthe, resulting in its turn from a confluence of the streams of Peybaron, Ferron and Villeneuve, to the east of the Saint-Laurent and Benon. Before joining the Gironde, the Jalle du Nord crosses the Beychevelle marshes and the Lauret fens which in ancient times were a centre of witchcraft in Médoc. To the north is the stream of Juillac, which acts as a border

between the vineyard of Château Léoville Las Cases and the Château Latour of the Pauillac appellation. About 16 hectares of land in Saint-Julien is owned by the Pauillac *crus*. The wine produced on this land is described as AOC Pauillac. To the west the limits of the appellation are marked by the Riou which flows into the Jalle du Nord and marks the limit of the commune.

When we say that Médoc means 'in the middle of the water' (*in medio aquae*) we do not immediately realize how true this is. All the great Médoc appellations are crossed by a network of waterways. Médoc is the Venice of the wine world but without canals or palaces.

▲ *Another form of traditional fishing uses a circular net which is lowered from cabins built on stilts. White shrimp and mullet are caught in this way.*

◄ *Two large streams drain the waters from the plateaux of Saint-Laurent. They are the Jalle du Nord and the Chenal du Milieu, which form small channels on the left bank of the estuary, crossing the Beychevelle marsh. Recently much work has been done on them, including the installation of a system of locks to avoid flooding during high tides.*

The Saint-Julien vineyard is centred on a church tower which raises a ramrod of white stone in the geographical centre of wine-producing Médoc. It is also, however, situated, in the modern sense of the term *appellation d'origine*, at the centre of a perfect hydrological network. This is what René Pijassou calls the 'insular model', although he applies this term more at the level of the *cru* than at the level of the region. A glance at the geological map of the Saint-Julien territory will help us to understand the individuality of the appellation. This appellation is not completely contained within the borders of the commune. A few isolated parcels of land are situated in Pauillac to the north, in Saint-Laurent to the west and in Cussac to the south. Their inclusion in the Saint-Julien appellation occurred in the initial land registry of certain classified *crus* which included a few scattered parcels of land. They have been assimilated into the main appellation development, while on the other hand certain estates to the south of Pauillac are considered to be owners of land at Saint-Julien. The major châteaux thus have an advantage over the producers who bor-

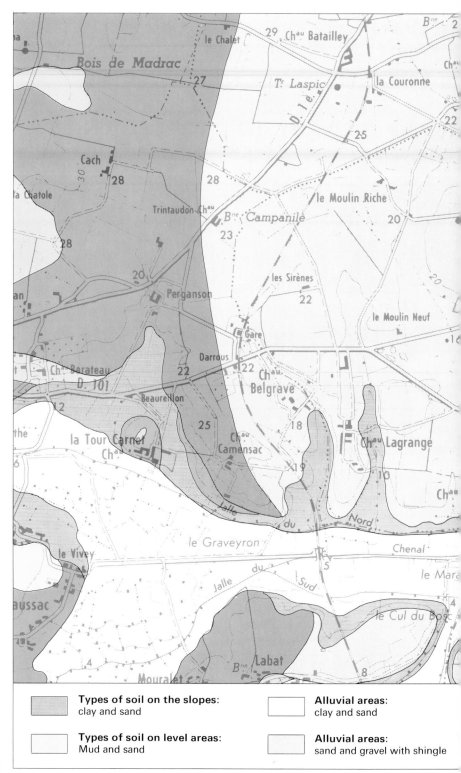

Types of soil on the slopes:
clay and sand

Alluvial areas:
clay and sand

Types of soil on level areas:
Mud and sand

Alluvial areas:
sand and gravel with shingle

Daubos
Ch⁴ᵘ Latour
Jeville
15
Ch⁴ᵘ Pichon-Lalande
de
D. 2
16
St.-Julien-
-Beychevelle
PORT DE
St.-JULIEN
16
Ch⁴ᵘ Leoville
Ch⁴ᵘ Talbot
le Tasta
D. 101 e
Ch⁴ᵘ
langoz
la Mouline
3
13
Ch⁴ᵘ du Glana
Ch⁴ᵘ Beaucaillou
Ch⁴ᵘ St.-Pierre
16
15
Beychevelle
la
Prade
D. 2
D. 101
Port de
Beychevelle
arose
Ch⁴ᵘ Beychevelle
Prés Lauret
5
le Bourdieu
3
Bouey P.
Pont de l'Archevêque
Milieu
2
4
chevelle
Ch⁴ᵘ Lanessan
Parat.
Ch⁴ᵘ Lachesnay
Ste-Gème
Despartins
17
ets
Bécard

0   500   1000 m

Alluvial areas:
gravel and sand

Lakeside (lacustral)
chalk and limestone

Marine limestone
with fossils

Marine chalk and
limestone

© IGN BRGM J.L SA Librairie NATHAN

35

der on these 'reclassified' parcels of land. While the border between the territories of Cussac and Beychevelle is clearly marked by the Chenal du Milieu and the Jalle du Nord, ending in the Beychevelle marsh, the situation is not the same in the west where the Riou forms only a fragile frontier. The AOC wines of Saint-Julien have been delineated in a restricted and protectionist way. The major part of the good wine-producing territories of Saint-Laurent could have been joined with Saint-Julien, as Arsac was joined with Margaux. Objectively speaking the difference in average prices between the AOC Saint-Julien wines and the AOC Haut-Médoc wines that make up the production of Saint-Laurent is excessive, considering the difference in quality between the two communes. However, as we noticed in most of the wine-producing territories in Bordeaux, it is extremely difficult to establish definitive limits for the origin of wine.

As it exists, the Saint-Julien appellation offers a fine homogenous quality which might be damaged by extending the territory. The best part of the land is contained in a triangle whose base runs from west to east for about 5 kilometres. There we can find, almost in a line running parallel with the Jalle du Nord, the estates of Châteaux Lagrange, Gruaud-Larose, Branaire and Beychevelle. Existing on the same pebbly, alluvial soil, the châteaux of La Tour-Carnet, Camensac and Belgrave which are situated at Saint-Laurent could well have been assimilated within the previous group. Meeting a right angle at Beychevelle we follow the short side of the triangle along the estuary as far as the village of Saint-Julien and the Juillac stream, a distance of about 3.5 kilometres, passing on the way the châteaux of Ducru-Beaucaillou, Langoa and the three Léoville establishments (Las Cases, Poyferré and Barton). The middle of the hypotenuse is marked by Château Talbot, whose vineyards stretch along a fine slope right in the centre of the appellation. The north-west sector outside the triangle is set on a plateau with a sandy, gravelly soil. It is less outstanding for wine production.

The origins of the parish of Saint-Julien go back to about the seventh century. Its exact name was Saint-Julien de Rinhac (or Rignac). The present official designation of the commune, which dates officially from 1938, is Saint-Julien-Beychevelle. It was not a question of combining two communes, as Beychevelle was never an entire parish, nor was it an administrative area. Rather, it came about because of a decree issued under the *ancien régime*. Quite simply, the territory was better represented by an association of the names of the two principal villages in the commune. The international fame of Beychevelle was an extra argument in favour of this union. In contrast, another parish existed until the nineteenth century to the north of Saint-Julien de Rignac. Built between the seventh and eighth centuries, the church of Saint-Maubert (later called Saint-Mambert and Saint-Lambert) was a subsidiary living to that of Saint-Julien. In fact the church was dedicated to Saint-Mamert, Bishop of Vienne (Isère) who lived in the fifth century and was the creator of the annual ceremony of Rogation. Saint Mamert is also one of the three redoubtable *saints de glace*, patron saints of the frost which causes considerable concern to the wine-producers during the rust-coloured moons of May, often leading to morning frosts.

The village known today as Saint-Lambert has been joined to Pauillac. If local history had prevailed – Saint-Lambert having originally been a subsidiary of Saint-Julien – the famous Château Latour would now be included in the Saint-Julien appellation and the latter

would have boasted a classified *1ᵉ cru* at the registration of 1855. The form of the plants on the gravelly terraces gives a greater sense of continuity from Beychevelle to the south of Pauillac than from Saint-Lambert to the Jalle du Breuil, the northern limit of the Pauillac appellation.

In other words the AOC Pauillac area contains two distinct zones, one to the south and the other to the north of the town. The difference between vineyards such as Bages, Batailley, Pichon and Latour and their immediate neighbours of Saint-Julien is much less pronounced than the differences between themselves and their counterparts in the northern part of Pauillac such as Lafite, Mouton and Pontet-Canet. Opinionated wine enthusiasts raise a smile when they claim to prefer the wines of Pauillac to those of Saint-Julien, or the other way round. (Particularly because, as I have mentioned earlier, the wine of Saint-Julien is harvested at Pauillac and vice versa!) Of the great Médoc appellations, those with the most individual characteristics in their ecology are respectively Margaux and Saint-Estèphe. At the centre of the region, Saint-Julien and Pauillac have numerous characteristics in common. That is why, when blind tastings of the great wines of Haut-Médoc are arranged, a verdict of *'centre Médoc'* is less risky than guessing at a distinction between Saint-Julien and Pauillac. In this context the wines of Saint-Estèphe and Margaux are easier to differentiate. If we choose the traditional position of north versus south, the northern wines of Pauillac can be similar to the wines of Saint-Estèphe, while most of the wines of Saint-Julien back up the southern argument in favour of Margaux wines. However, the frontiers of Pauillac-south and Saint-Julien-north will always remain rather close and it would be rash to make definite distinctions between the two.

Whatever the arguments, however, the wines of Saint-Mambert-de-Reignac come under the Pauillac appellation. I think I should emphasize the common origins of the parishes of Saint-Julien and Saint-Mambert, which were originally both called de Reignac. We may also note that between the regions of Margaux and Bourgeais, many places on opposite sides of the river bear the same name. Thus, Reignac is exactly opposite Saint-Julien, on the right bank, 18 kilometres from Blaye. It is difficult to draw conclusions and make comparisons. This would seem though to confirm the numerous exchanges which were made across the estuary at a time when local navigation was the main method of communication. I would even put forward the theory that this similarity in names goes back to the Gallo-Roman period and that a certain 'Renius', a contemporary of Ausone, owned villas on either side of the river.

The small town of Saint-Julien and the village of Beychevelle are the

Categories	1874	1922	1949	1969	1982
	Number	*Number*	*Number*	*Number*	*Number*
	Volume in tonneaux	*Volume in tonneaux*	*Volume in tonneaux*	*Volume in tonneaux*	*Volume in tonneaux*
Crus classés	13	13	12	11	11
	1245	1650	1275	1840	2310
Crus bourgeois	4	11	11	4	6
	66	230	241	358	570
Crus artisans	28	12	14	16	16
	348	153	122	271	396
Small growers	15	15	15	15	5
	45	45	45	45	25
Totals	60	51	52	46	38
	1704	2078	1683	2514	3301

two components of the appellation. The rest of the habitat is scattered in modest hamlets around the châteaux. The properties have been carved out from the vineyards in a very precise way, and isolated parcels of land are less frequent than in the Margaux appellation. Concentrated production has also taken place: there are very few small wine-producers in existence today. This development can be traced in the successive editions of *Bordeaux et ses vins* by Féret (see table above).

We can see from the table that Saint-Julien's wine production has doubled in a century, while the number of small producers has decreased by a third. These statistics are even more significant when they are adjusted by the addition of *2e vins* from certain *grands crus*, which regularly declassify a part of their production. The owners sell large quantities of wine produced on their estates under a different brand. This is the practice at present with most of the major appellations. At Saint-Julien many *crus classés* possess at least one reserve brand.

If we examine the nominal production of *crus classés* during the last century, we note a certain disproportion in the increase in yield. The champion of greater yields is Château Talbot, which has increased production from 100 to almost 400 *tonneaux*. Next comes Léoville

Poyferré who declared a production of 80 *tonneaux* in 1874 and 200 in 1982. Many have doubled their production, including Léoville Las Cases, Léoville Barton, Gruaud-Larose, Ducru-Beaucaillou and Beychevelle. The remainder produce a more or less constant volume of wine which means that the areas of their vineyards have tended to become smaller as yield per hectare is much greater than a hundred years ago. We estimate about 25 hectolitres per hectare as an average yield of a *grand cru* at the beginning of this century under optimum conditions. The basic yield with regard to the INAO for Saint-Julien is not 40 hectolitres. There have been occasions, however, when the association of appellation wine-producers requests authority to declare a yield of 70 hectolitres! During the last thirty years the Médoc vineyard in general and that of Saint-Julien in particular have been working towards a greater yield. Such an increase agrees with the average figure for all Bordeaux wines which amounted to a total of 29.82 hectolitres per hectare in the decade 1950–9 and increased to 46.10 hectolitres per hectare during the years 1970–9. Although there have been certain years when wine-producers have succeeded in producing a very high quantity by harvesting grapes of first quality, it would seem that in general the average yield is now about 45 hectolitres per hectare.

In 1855 there were thirteen Saint-Julien *crus classés* and the number is now eleven. The appellation cannot sell the *1ᵉ cru* but the jury of the Universal Exhibition awarded Saint-Julien six *2ᵉ crus classés*. There follows a list of the classifications for Saint-Julien.

	Name in 1855 classification	Present name
2ᵉ crus		
Léoville	*Marquis de Las Cazes*	Léoville Las Cases
	Baron de Poyféré	Léoville Poyferré
	Barton	Léoville Barton
Gruaud Laroze	*de Bethman*	
	Bᵒⁿ Sarget de	Gruaud-Larose
	Boisgerard	
Ducru Beaucaillou		Ducru-Beaucaillou
3ᵉ crus		
Lagrange		Lagrange
Langoa		Langoa
4ᵉ crus		
Saint-Pierre	*Bontemps Dubary*	Saint-Pierre
	Vve Roullet	
	Vve Galloupeau	
Talbot		Talbot
Du Luc		Branaire
Beychevele		Beychevelle

The award for the most remarkable increase in quality during the last century must be given to Beychevelle, which in 1855 was the last of the classified Saint-Julien wines and has now risen to the level of *2ᵉ crus*. The five authentic *2ᵉ crus* are involved in a serious but dignified competition for prestige. In the 1982 edition the *Bordeaux et ses vins* (classified in order of merit for each commune) mentions Ducru-Beaucaillou in first position followed by Léoville Las Cases, Gruaud-Larose, Léoville Poyferré and Léoville Barton. Châteaux Beychevelle and Talbot are described as being very superior for their classification. On the contrary Branaire does not even merit the word 'very'. (Personally I find Branaire very, very good.)

When growth is too rapid, it is advisable to cut off the 'suckers', growth of which will detract from the fruit-bearing branches.

However, the supreme award for any appellation must be given to Château Gloria, developed over the last forty years by Henri Martin, mayor of Saint-Julien. There is much to say about this wine and I shall go into it more fully a little later in the book. In 1855 Gloria existed only as a name in the Land Register for a parcel of ground at Beychevelle. Today, although not being a *cru* of great age, Château Gloria enjoys a universal reputation. *Bordeaux et ses vins* describes it as 'being possibly worthy of a new classification'. In other words, Gloria, which has already been awarded many medals in regional and national exhibitions, is waiting for the next Universal Exhibition to see its merits fully recognized. In 1973 Gloria almost followed in the path of the Mouton when Philippe de Rothschild alone succeeded in gaining a *premier* classification. However, a general revision of the classifications would have caused too much of a stir in the towns of Médoc.

No one knows when, where or how the next classification of the Gironde wines will take place. The Universal Exhibition in Paris, which was planned for 1989, has collapsed after a certain amount of activity. It seems to me that this exhibition would have been an ideal platform for the establishment of the new hierarchy for all the wines of France, although I am not convinced of the economic advantage of these very high-level competitions. Whatever the circumstances, Château Gloria has been a wonderful success for Henri Martin, who never ceases in his efforts to improve his wine.

The son of a cooper, Henri Martin was *maître de chai* at Château Saint-Pierre. The functions of manager and director of the *chais* are extremely important to the great wine estates. At Saint-Julien and at Beychevelle, generations of *maîtres de chai* have succeeded each other and have become famous local names, comparable to those ships' captains whose skill (and occasionally good luck) made the fortunes of the ship-owners. Nowadays the *maîtres de chai* come from a new school. They have been trained in the science of oenology according to the maxims of 'Monseigneur' Peynaud. They carry out their responsible work with the help of laboratories and the advice of highly qualified specialists, supported by sophisticated scientific techniques. Only thirty years ago, however, the work of vinification and wine-storing depended on another type of science, whose principal technique was the use of the ear, the eye, the nose and the mouth. Yes, I have included the ear, which takes note of the hissing in the vats at the beginning of fermentation or the bubbling of the must when the temperature increases too rapidly. The eye judges not only the colour of the wine but also its clarity after racking and the problems which may arise in the springtime. When he brings his new wine into the *chai,* 45 the *maître* should be able to tell what the weather will be like merely by glancing round the bungs in his casks. As for the nose and the mouth ... I shall leave you to judge their capabilities.

Like cellar rats, *maîtres de chai* can be either from the town or from the country. The Barton family, who still own the Châteaux Léoville Barton and Langoa at Saint-Julien and who were associated with the famous firm of Barton and Guestier, wine shippers in Bordeaux, were famous for the excellence of their *maîtres de chai*, both in the châteaux and at Chartons. The painter and engraver Gustave de Galard has created a superb portrait of the *maître de chai* of this trading company in about 1823. The engraving still serves as a greeting card which is sent to all the Bordeaux gentry.

Less well known is the character portrait written by Galard himself.

Except in Bordeaux, no one seems to know exactly what a *maître de chai* is. It is not clear whether it is a profession or a duty and if we look in the dictionary the problem is not solved, as the word *chais* is a local word that replaces the one we would use for cellar (*cellier*). The *maîtres de chai* are chosen from the coopers for their application to work, their intelligence and their honesty. They are chosen by the employers from those working in the reception, the production and the maintenance departments. Once they are established in this function, which is of the greatest importance to the employers, they gain much authority over those workers with whom they were previously on equal terms. It is noticeable that when a *maître de chai* is among the coopers, the bargemen, the general workers and the wagoners, he has an authority which no other team leader possesses and his orders are carried out to the letter.

His power and influence do not stop there, however. He is responsible for checking the wines purchased by his employers. It is quite something to see the efficient way in which a *maître de chai* places his taster in the casks that the timid owner has brought to him, almost spitting the wine in his face after his impeccable palate has made the judgement. This is not all, though: when the seller, almost rigid with fright, has undergone this severe test, he has to undergo yet another one which is intended to establish the accurate capacity of the casks. The inevitable *velte* or capacity-measuring instrument is plunged into each cask and is pushed around inside in such an expert manner that it is very unusual for the seller not to allow some small reduction in price.

These reductions in price are, of course, perfectly justified and it

G. de Galard   *Lith. de Gaulon.*

Maître de Chai.

An engraving of a maître de chai *by Gustave de Galard taken from the portrait belonging to the House of Barton and Guestier. This picture is without doubt the most famous representation of an inhabitant of Bordeaux. Gustave de Galard did several other illustrations connected with the* grands crus *of Médoc; the original editions are very much in demand today and fetch high prices.*

would be useless to protest as the *maître* has stipulated them. The man in the picture is shown at the moment when he is examining old wines during their racking process. He is not at all an ideal being. We have taken the opportunity to have a painting based on him to decorate the office of one of the most reliable wine shippers in this town. A great distinction won by long service and irreproachable honesty!

We no longer find *maîtres de chai* wearing three-cornered hats, straight coats and long waistcoats over leather aprons. Such people, family men, who set an example of hard work, honesty, impartiality and obedience, now seem far too Gothic. We strongly doubt that in the future there will be many portraits of *maîtres de chai* in the offices of Bordeaux.

Gustave de Galard was quite correct as far as the *maîtres de chai* in town are concerned. There are very few of them who have passed into posterity. However, the *maîtres de chai* of the *grands crus* still remain celebrities. They are photographed from behind, from in front and in profile as they inspect, inhale, taste and expectorate. Like great athletes after an important match, they give interviews during harvest-time and when the new vintage is announced. They appear on television. They sign autographs for tourists on labels from the châteaux. Their employers even invite them sometimes to sign 'personalized' letters which are sent to the most important of their private customers. In a word, they are stars and some of them even have press-cutting books which would make Charles Aznavour or Michel Platini turn green with envy.

The 'Gothic' style has certainly evolved in 150 years. When they carry out a tasting, some of them raise a finger in the air while they sniff in to their glass. Their vocabulary has been enriched by specialized terms which their local accent makes more persuasive – rather like Michel Oliver describing a new recipe. However, apart from the technical control which is exercised during vinification, the technique used by the *maîtres de chai* in producing their wine has remained more or less the same for more than a century. The main processes involved are topping up, racking, blending and fining.

Topping up means filling the cask completely. During the first year of ageing in the new wine *chai*, the barrels are placed with their bungs on top but without being hermetically sealed. For most of the time the whole of the bung on the side of the cask is closed by a large glass marble which blocks the hole without sealing it. This hole must be kept perfectly clean and the evaporation of the wine must be corrected.

This latter operation is carefully carried out by men who replace the quantity of wine missing in each cask so that the level rises as far as the bung. By tradition, a cask and its fractional parts, that is a half, a quarter and an eighth, are used continuously to supply the quantity of wine necessary for topping up.

Racking is the process of separating the lees from the 'fine wine'. This decanting operation is carried out by means of bellows that compress the air in the cask about to be racked. Then the wine is slowly transferred into another cask. When its level reaches the bung placed in the end of the cask, the person carrying out the racking waits for a while

---

The worker in the chai *tops up each cask during the first year of the maturing process. He uses a topping up vessel which is a sort of watering can with a long spout on which is a candle.*

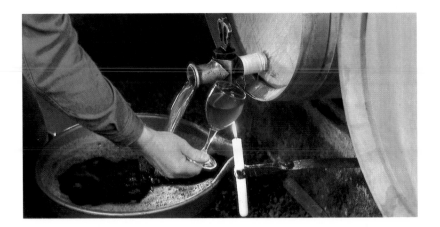

and then finishes the job by emptying the remainder of the 'clear' wine into a small basin, constantly checking the clarity in a glass held before a candle. As soon as the first traces of the lees appear, he says *'Lève'* and his companion returns the cask to the horizontal. In order to make racking easier, the Bordeaux casks have two holes at the base. The second, which is lower than the first, is called the *esquive*.

It is of interest to note that the true meaning of the term 'fine wine' is really 'racked to fine quality'. During the period when wine merchants in Bordeaux received delivery of their purchases in casks, it was forbidden to transport the wine 'on the lees'. The merchants' orders stipulated that the wines (for example Château Léoville Poyferré) should be delivered 'commercially acceptable and in good condition, with correct taste, full and racked'. The lees were then collected and withdrawn some months later. Formerly, in the case of *grands crus*, it was the custom that the 'wines from the lees' were the personal reserve of the *maître de chai*. To those with a taste for tannic wines, they can be delicious.

Blending is certainly the most important operation in the production of a *grand vin*. This term also has its own special meaning. The owner and his *maître de chai* make a selection of the best *cuvées* from a harvest according to the success of particular vines in a particular area of the vineyard. We should emphasize that Bordeaux wines are made from several vines, in contrast to those of several other wine-producing regions.

▲ *A candle is still the best source of light for the racking process, as it has a concentrated centre. Here we see racking being carried out at Château Lagrange.*

During racking, the wine is taken from the vats and put in casks (preferably new). After a few months of close inspection those batches of wine chosen for the grand vin *are returned to the vats for blending and are then transferred to oak barrels. This process is illustrated at Château Léoville-Poyferré.* ▶

The variety of territories and of vines is an essential factor in the creation of a *grand vin*, which is really a mixture of these different components. This is why a *grand cru* must really come from a considerable surface area in order to achieve its high quality. This, of course, depends on the territories being the best possible, and the creation of the *premier vin* or *grand vin* being the result of a very demanding choice. This is not always the case. Personally I find that the practice of *secondes marques*, which is becoming more general, is an excellent development so long as it allows the main brand of the *cru* to have the best quality production. Here the role of the *maître de chai* is absolutely vital as he, better than anyone else, is capable of judging the future of his creation.

Fining is the best method of clarifying wine. Various products, more or less chemical, may be used but nothing can really replace using egg white, a practice which first appeared in Médoc towards the beginning of the eighteenth century. After separating the whites from the yolks, the former are beaten until stiff, using from four to six eggs per cask according to the tannic content of the wine. They are then poured into the cask and the contents are 'beaten' – that is, a bunch of horse hair

attached to an iron rod is slowly agitated inside the cask. In the local Bordeaux dialect this fining was called *fouettage*. This is how Magdeleine Duheron of Bordeaux described the operation in her *Livre de raison*:

> The process of *fouettage* usually takes place in April for the new wines, and when a cask is needed for the new supplies. Normally 12 whites of fresh eggs are used with a little yolk and some broken shell, together with a pinch of salt for the Bordeaux cask. *Fouettage* makes the wines more delicate but tires them if used too often. It is necessary in the spring when the wine is working. Checking is done either with a silver goblet or a crystal glass held before a flame. The wine is left to rest for 20–25 days. Sometimes after the *fouettage* and a first racking the wine does not always appear very fine. A second racking is often necessary a month and a half after the first. It is prudent to use sulphur in each racking. However, discretion

At Château Branaire the maître de chai, *Marcel Renon, prepares the fining for a cask, using fresh egg whites.*

should be used otherwise the colour of the wine is ruined. When you do the vatting and you are halfway through the process, you should add as many handfuls of flowers of salt as there are casks of wine.

At the time this was written the wines would macerate in the vat together with the grapeskins for more than a month, sometimes even for two months. The wines contained much more tannin than nowadays and this explains the quantity of eggs needed for fining. Ageing in cask lasted from two to four years and two finings were necessary in order to remove enough of the 'heavy substances'. The technique of fining, however, has scarcely changed today except that we no longer add 'a little yolk and some broken shell with a pinch of flowers of salt', and that the time recommended for fining is generally 45 days. The tracery of egg white that rises to the top of the cask after the *fouettage* will slowly descend, and as it coagulates the tiny bubbles will disappear, carrying down with them the impurities that are suspended in the wine. It should be noted that the tannins from the newly cut oak planks in the cask help in this coagulation. This is one of the reasons why every year *grands crus* renew either a part or their entire stock of barrels. We should also note that the curve of a cask in the horizontal position preserves a volume of approximately 10 litres (that is, a little less than 5 per cent of the contents) which corresponds to the average quantity of lees deposited. To close this short series of observations based on the laws of nature let us note that fining is generally done in April when the vine starts budding and when chickens begin to lay eggs again in preparation for Easter. A *cru* producing 200 *tonneaux* of wine will need about 4000 eggs for the fining. At this time of year, it is popular to eat many omelettes, preferably with wild garlic... omelettes made, however, without egg whites as these have already been used in the fining.

We know that albumen oxidizes metals, and will even tarnish silver. In all of the *grands crus* of Médoc the egg whites are beaten in a wooden bowl, using a small whisk made of heather twigs. This instrument which is called a *bontemps*, is the inspiration for the name of the Commanderie du Bontemps du Médoc et des Graves, of which Henri Martin was the principal founder. This is why it seems a suitable moment to speak of it with reference to the Saint-Julien appellation.

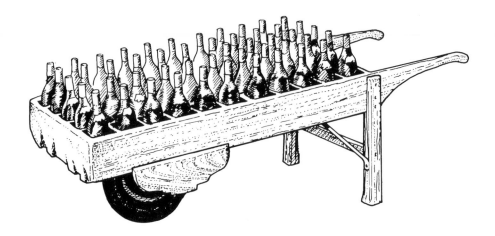

The robe of the Commanderie du Bontemps de Médoc et des Graves is Bordeaux-coloured velvet. Not really the colour of a Bordeaux, however. It is rather the colour of the must of the Merlot grape, in its great years after nineteen days of maceration. It is a fine colour. On the right shoulder a pale green pleated band of satin symbolizes the young shoots of the vine. A large pierced bronze badge constitutes the insignia of the order and a miniature of this is offered to newly elected members at the installation ceremony. All this is very becoming, as indeed are the robes of the other 82 fraternities of wine-producers which exist in France and Navarre. Have you noticed, incidentally, that there is never a chivalric order without a headdress? As far as I know, no Bacchic order has had the temerity to reintroduce the wig, classic symbol of the magistracy, but there is no order in existence without a hat. Be it the cap of the president of the Law Court or the three-cornered hat of Louis XIII, a hat confers dignity on the wearer. The hat worn by the Commanderie du Bontemps is inspired by the wooden bowl in which the egg whites are beaten before the fining process. Its shape resembles a salad bowl. It is made from the same velvet as the robe, and the crown is made of white tulle, representing the whites of egg. The local name, peculiar to Médoc, for the bowl upon which the hat its based is *desquet*. It inspired Raymond Brard, poet of the fraternity at its inauguration, to create a Rabelaisian

▲ *After being separated from the yolks, the egg whites are beaten until stiff in a wooden bowl called a* bontemps, *or in dialect a* desquet. *A small heather whisk is used. The whites are then poured into a cask for fining and are briskly agitated with a* fouet.

The chai *of Château Langoa has a fine vaulted crypt.* ▶

Raymond Brard and Henri Martin, the two senior members of the Commanderie du Bontemps de Médoc et des Graves.

character called Jean-Odule Paulin d'Esquet as the 'Order' founder, whose august and venerable origin is lost in the mists of the Middle Ages. I like this well-chosen touch of fantasy. Perhaps one day I shall do some serious historical research on the gentleman and publish a book on his life!

The first fraternity of wine-producers, Les Chevaliers du Tastevin, was created in 1934, though it was not until after the war that it attracted the attention of the press. Henri Martin was rather partial to local publicity and secretly admired the loquaciousness of the Burgundians. He thought that what they were doing was admirable. In 1948, a group of people from Saint-Emilion founded the 'Jurade'. Martin could resist the temptation no longer. He had a friend from his military days called Henri Francotte who looked after Château Beychevelle and who augmented his income by doing extra work here and there. He was hired to organize the inauguration of the Jurade by M. Demund, who was to Bordeaux what the wine merchant Lenôtre was to Paris. Aware of the curiosity of his friend Martin, Francotte brought back with him everything he could find in the way of documents. From then on Martin was unstoppable, especially when three days later his assistant, Emile Liquard, telephoned him and said: 'What are you getting up to? We only read about Saint-Emilion in the press! What about Médoc ... What's happening about our region?

What are you waiting for? . . . There must be something you can do to get these people moving!' This conversation was the last straw, and thus was born, in 1949, the fraternity of Médoc. Henri Martin had some good contacts, among whom were M. Lucas and M. Seurin, presidents of the Caves coopératives de Bégadan et de Pauillac; M. Marjary, administrator for Mouton-Rothschild; and Pierre Ginestet, who was always ready to give a helping hand. They intended initially to found a sort of super tourist board. Henri Martin agreed, but he was not entirely satisfied. He discussed his obsession with his friend Raymond Brard who was then engineer for the Highways Board of Saint-Laurent and a local history enthusiast with a tendency to be anti-conformist. One day, while they were lunching in a restaurant in Pauillac, Martin and Brard were discussing the problem with the help of a suitable bottle of Château Gloria. Suddenly, over the cheese, Brard said enthusiastically: 'Well, Henri, you are not going to tell me that there is nothing in Médoc that cannot act as a vehicle for your project? . . . Look at the Burgundians — they have started their own fraternity. Can't you do something to trump their card? I am sure there is a solution we can find . . .' Feeling that he was being unjustly accused, Martin replied: 'I am not sure, but why don't we use as a symbol one of the various utensils connected with wine-making? Perhaps we could use the *bontemps*.' Brard asked what that was and Martin explained, saying in conclusion: 'In the local dialect it is called a *desquet*.' Brard rose like Archimedes leaving the bath, heroic and impressive, and declared: 'Henri, that is a stroke of genius, I always knew it. Let us drink a toast to the companions of the Bontemps de Médoc and to Théodule Desquet, their ancestor!' A little later Brard discovered that Desquet's real name was Jean-Odule Paulin and that his descendant's exact title was 'Commandeur'.

Henri Martin arranged the administration of the Order which was supported from the very beginning by members of all the estates producing *1e crus*. He admits today that this was a major factor in his success. 'These people needed us least but their participation from the beginning had a very strong snowball effect.' Roger Dourthe, Edouard Gasqueton, Jean-Charles and André Cazes and Armand Achille-Fould, apart from those whom I have already mentioned, were among the founders of the Commanderie. The first Grand Master was Gasqueton, owner of Château Calon-Ségur at Saint-Estèphe.

Raymond Brard, an inventive and cultured man who preferred to prepare the *fêtes* rather than take part in them, wrote the medieval

texts. Helped by some of the best *crus* he made the meetings of the Commanderie very lively. The local aristocracy were amazed by his spectacular ventures. It is true that Raymond Brard was not always the most subtle of men, but he had enormous talent for arranging the Bacchic meetings of the Médoc notables. In contrast to the Chevaliers du Tastevin, who meet by tradition at the château of Clos Vougeot, the Commandeurs move from château to château, of which there is no shortage to choose from. The regular meetings take place during the feast of Saint-Vincent, the *Fête de la Fleur* and the *Ban des Vendanges*. However, on important occasions the inauguration ceremonies can take place at any time in any of the estates of Médoc or Graves. (The Graves region joined the Commanderie during the sixties.)

Having listened to the candidate's inauguration speech the Grand Council of the Order agrees to his admission with the ritual formula, *Pot intrar* (He may enter). Armand Achille-Fould, owner of Château Beychevelle, who followed Edouard Gasqueton, was an admirable Grand Master of the Commanderie, whereas neither Henri Martin nor André Cazes (Château Lynch-Bages at Pauillac) could spare the time or the effort to handle the administration. However, after the death of Achille-Fould, Henri Martin took over the responsibilities of Grand Master which he still holds. He is the son of a cooper from the village of Beychevelle and has done great work for the wines of his 'parish'. He has a talent for public relations, is very eloquent and has travelled throughout the world promoting the wines of Saint-Julien (Gloria was, of course, never forgotten on the way). His efforts benefited all of Médoc and Bordeaux wines in general, as he was president of the Conseil Interprofessionnel du Vin de Bordeaux (CIVB). Like Jacques Chaban-Delmas at Bordeaux, Henri Martin has been mayor of Saint-Julien since 1947. He decided to stand for the local elections following a bet which he made with Jean-Charles Cazes, the present mayor and regional councillor of Pauillac. He stood as a candidate for 'local union' in a municipality which was socialist-communist, and for which the father of Jean-Eugène Borie, owner of the Château Ducru-Beaucaillou, was also a candidate. Henri Martin was the only person elected at the first ballot. Borie withdrew from the election and Martin was duly elected. Since then the 'mayor–wine-producer' of Saint-Julien has never been beaten.

The mayor of Saint-Julien before the Popular Front was Désiré Cordier, founder of the famous commercial house and owner of Châteaux Gruaud-Larose and Talbot. Cordier was also a man with a talent for publicity. In 1934 he organized in Saint-Julien the *Fête de la longévité* (the festival of long life). He had noticed that at Saint-Julien, and in Médoc generally, the life expectancy was much higher than the national average. For a population of 1272 inhabitants he discovered that there was one diamond wedding for every 13 golden weddings, that is, 14 couples who had been married for more than half a century. He compared local and national statistics, as can be seen below.

Per 100,000 inhabitants

Ages	France	Médoc
60–64 years	4661	6259
65–69 years	3644	5000
70–79 years	4359	6550
80 years +	1053	1981
Total	13,717	19,790

These statistics showed that in the 57 communes of Médoc, for every 100,000 inhabitants there were 6073 more 'elderly persons' than in the rest of France. This meant that there was a 45 per cent higher life expectancy. Cordier concluded that it would be 'lacking respect towards our national drink if we failed to draw attention to such an important comparison in favour of good wines.' He made a census of all the elderly couples in Médoc and, including those whom he had already counted in his own commune, he arrived at a total of 407. 'The conclusion, supported by statistics, is that Médoc, and in particular Saint-Julien, is the most favourable region for octogenarians, which proves most decisively that wine – of course good wine – is as I have already said, the "elixir for long life".' Armed with such irrefutable proof Cordier invited Albert Lebrun, president of the Third Republic, to visit Médoc and appreciate the virtues of the elixir. The presidential train which arrived at the station of Saint-Laurent-Saint-Julien was greeted with much pomp and ceremony. The route to the square in Saint-Julien was closely guarded. An enormous marquee had been erected opposite the house of the deputy mayor, M. Jules Billa, where all the entertainment necessary for such an occasion had been prepared. There were three banquets that day involving 1400 people. First there was the official luncheon, during the course of which a Château Gruaud-Larose 1834 was served. Henri Martin was responsible for the wines and it was he who served the hundred-year-old wine at the table of Président Lebrun. Next to the presidential marquee

were the four hundred-odd couples who had been married for fifty years, who were not slow in raising their glasses and enjoying themselves immensely. A little way away, and a little later, the Security Service was entertained. Each member received a 'luncheon voucher' and a personal bottle when he sat down at table. No accidents were reported.

One year later, in 1935, the association of wine-producers of the commune registered the name of Saint-Julien. After the law of 1936 concerning AOC wines, Saint-Julien was officially included without any particular difficulty and the vineyard of Saint-Julien and Beychevelle was thus confirmed among the first rank of the most celebrated communes in Médoc.

Among the legends that supply raw material for wine journalists and writers throughout the world, the origin that was claimed for the name of Beychevelle (Baysse Velle) is one of the bestsellers. *Bordeaux et ses vins*, the more than a century-old 'bible' of Bordeaux wines that no amateur or professional can afford to ignore, still describes Château Beychevelle in the following terms: 'The name of Beychevelle (*baisse-voile*) comes from the salute made in the past by ships sailing past the castle of the Duke of Epernon, who was then grand admiral of France.'

President Lebrun leaving the train at Saint-Laurent station where he was welcomed by Désiré Cordier, at that time mayor of Saint-Julien-Beychevelle.

I do not know why this phrase makes me think of the operetta *The White Horse Inn* in which there is a song: 'I shall take you away in my pretty boat...' but I shall invite you to hoist your sails and weigh anchor for a journey through history.

II

It is high time for the mystery shrouding the legend of 'Baysse Velle' to be revealed. For this version of its origins, as it is told to little children by their grandparents, is nothing more than a fantasy. It has no more substance than the life and work of Paulin d'Esquet, the founder of the Commanderie whom we have previously mentioned. However, I must admit that I like the romance of the story: the fine men-of-war and the merchant ships all lowering their sails as a gesture of respect to the Duke of Epernon as he surveyed the scene from his balcony, while the duchess graciously waved her kerchief and, wiping away a furtive tear, said to her husband: 'My dear, don't you think it's sweet of them to lose time on our behalf?' 'Quite normal, my dear', the duke would reply in a majestic voice, 'the good manners of seafaring folk are proverbial and, after all, they know that I am the Admiral in the service of God and the King.' 'Yes my dear, you are noble, just and admirable', his wife would reply.

So, every type of ship, not only the French but also those flying the flag of England, Holland, Spain and the Romagna, would show their admiration by lowering their sails, while those who were badly brought up would lower their trousers and reveal their sterns, which shocked the duchess and made the children shriek with mirth.

Jean-Louis Nogaret de la Valette was born in 1554. He was the second son of Jean Nogaret and Jeanne de Saint-Lary de Bellegarde, his wife. His father came of a respectable family from upper Gascogny and held the post of *Maître de camp* of the French light cavalry as well as that of lieutenant-general for the King in Guyenne. During his youth Jean-Louis was called Caumont, after the ancient manorial home situated between Auch and Toulouse. He received a military education and gave early proof of his disposition for a military career. He gained the affection of King Henri III, becoming his favourite and being created the first Duke of Epernon. He was an ambitious, pushy opportunist and played an important part in state affairs, being one of the architects – sometimes at great risk – of the accession of Henri IV. Loaded with honours, riches and power, he was dominated by violent passions and consumed with excessive pride. He was a man of extremely strong character. In 1587, when he had already been awarded many honours, he married the last heiress of the powerful house of Grailly-Foix, Marguerite de Foix Candale. This was for him an extra piece of good fortune which he used with much ostentation, giving the most lavish receptions in the kingdom. That same year both the Duke of Joyeuse and the Maréchal de Bellegarde died at the battle of Coutras fighting the army of Henri of Navarre. The former shared with Jean-Louis de La Valette the royal favours of Henri III. The King wished to avoid having to grant or refuse the Duke of Guise the responsibilities carried out by Joyeuse so he entrusted them all to La Valette, who at the same time also inherited those of his cousin Bellegarde. Thus La Valette added to his own and his wife's coats of arms two additional lists of noble responsibilities which made him the premier duke of France.

Although I am certain to omit some of them, I give here details of the main titles of the duke: Jean-Louis Nogaret de La Valette, Duke of Epernon and La Valette, Knight of the King's Order, Peer and Admiral of France, First Gentleman of the King's Bedchamber, Major-General of the French Infantry, Governor of Normandy, Caen and of Havre de Grace, Governor of Saintonge, Angoumois and Pays d'Aunis, Governor of Metz and the Province, Governor and Lieutenant-General of the Duchy of Guyenne ... apologies for such a short list! But as well as all that he was also Prince of Buch, Lord of Lesparre, Count of Astarac, Foix, Montfort and Benauge, Viscount of Castillion, Baron of Cadillac, Vayres, Langon, Rions, Podensac, Castelnau, Plassac – and, finally, of Bayssevelle.

It should be noted that the Duke of Epernon was already Baron of Beychevelle when he was created Admiral of France by Henri III. In this context the legend of 'lowering the sails' will not stand up to the facts of French history. The etymology of Beychevelle goes back to the

Middle Ages. Local tradition, according to which the Admiral of La Valette, the Duke of Epernon, obliged passing ships to salute him, is a fairy-tale. Returning to the origins of Beychevelle, we should point out that La Valette never lived in this area. His main residence was the Château de Plassac, on the other side of the estuary, and the principal family seat was at the Château de Cadillac.

However, we should mention that Jean-Louis de La Valette bought the estate of Lesparre from the Maréchal Jacques de Matignon, his predecessor as Lieutenant-General of Guyenne. This brought with it the title of first baron of the province and the first place at the States General. After the Hundred Years War and the surrender of Bordeaux to the French crown, Médoc was claimed by five rival lords. These were Amanieu d'Albret, appointed by Charles VII; Gaston de Foix, appointed by Jeanne de Pressac; the famous Dunois, companion of Jeanne d'Arc, who spent a great deal of his spoils of war to buy several estates near Saint-Laurent (including the Château La Tour Carnet); Olivier de Coëtivry, who had also been promised the position by the King; and finally Pierre de Montferrant, who claimed the right through his mother, Isabeau de Preyssac. For half a century nobody knew exactly who owned what. The former lords of Lesparre, destitute and extradited, took refuge in England. In 1455 one of the family visited his ancestral lands but he was recognized and executed at Poitiers, without even having the time to climb the keep of the Château de Lesparre. The Maréchal de Matignon was Baron of Lamarque, whose estate bordered that of Castillion. He was a great soldier but rather bellicose, a characteristic which caused him to fall into disgrace at the court on several occasions. He settled in Médoc, on his estate, which he bought in 1593 from François de Foix de Candale, Duke of Rendan, Baron of Castelnau, Lamarque and Bayssevelle, a descendant of the most ancient family of English Guyenne. From his castle – served by three ports on the river, one of which was Beychevelle – he could easily command the blockade of Blaye, a garrison in the hands of religious devotees which gave much trouble by acts of piracy along the river. Six ships arrived to give help, while the king of Spain sent sixteen warships to help the besieged inhabitants. The Bordeaux fleet of six well-armed ships, under the command of Captain Lalimaille, took shelter off the coast of Médoc and left the English to fend for themselves, to the fury of the Maréchal de Matignon.

On Saturday 26 July 1597, dining in his Château de Lamarque, Matignon had an apoplectic fit while raising a glass of wine to his lips. His body was taken by river to Bordeaux where a ceremonial funeral was held. During the settlement of the estate, his children started to quarrel bitterly. Rushing to the help of this family afflicted with the problems of a large fortune, Jean-Louis de La Valette managed to buy the entire estate of Lesparre for a sum of 210,000 pounds and was delighted to acquire all the lands which had belonged to the ancestors of his wife, Jean, Gaston and Frédéric de Foix, Counts of Candale. He also acquired the 'rights of the Admiralty' which went with the peninsula, which must not be confused with his position as Admiral. The former gave him rights to the loot from shipwrecks which, for four centuries, had been the main source of income for the lords of Lesparre, both on the sea-coast and on the left bank of the estuary. Every wrecked ship and its cargo scattered on the beach; every bottle thrown into the sea; every cask of damp powder; everything down to the smallest piece of flotsam and jetsam had to be delivered to the lord of Lesparre. With respect to many reputable historians, now no longer with us, it is possible that the origin of the name of 'Lesparre' came from the trade of involuntary shipwrecking practised by the masters of Médoc.

Whatever the circumstances, it is a fact that the first Duke of Epernon, Admiral of France, claimed his dues of the Admiralty. Although he may not have obliged the ships leaving or entering the river to lower their sails, he insisted on collecting the enormous quantity of flotsam scattered between the Bassin d'Arcachon and the Pointe de Grave, on the Atlantic coast, and from this point as far as the Château de Lamarque on the Gironde side.

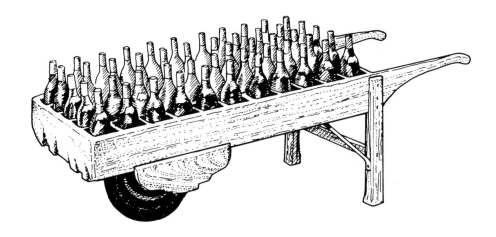

Jean-Louis Nogaret de la Valette, the first Duke of Epernon, was one of Henri III's favourites.

▶

IEAN LOUIS DE LA VALLETTE

DUC D'ESPERNON

Pair et
neral de
verneur et
General go
enne Ville et
Metz et pais

Colonel Ge
France Gou
Lieutenant
Le Roi en la
hadelle de
Messin

71

In 1603 a famous Italian gambler called Pimentel arrived in France and was presented at the court of Henri III. The court was always interested in amusing pastimes. Having been warned that the King was passionately fond of gambling, Pimentel arranged to have a large quantity of trick dice made of which he alone understood the irregularities. In this way he gained control of the game and made himself master of fortune. He was unbelievably skilled at winning. The King allowed him to do so, not at all annoyed that Pimentel succeeded in impoverishing certain of his courtiers whose wealth was very suspect. The Duke of Epernon was one of those from whom he won the largest amounts of money. In a few days and few games, Pimentel took from him all his ready cash and many of his jewels. For the equivalent of 20,000 crowns (the value of a fine baronial estate), he won from him a piece of ambergris, the largest piece known in Europe. Ambergris was very much in demand in all courts, where it was used as the base for traditional perfumes. Its animal, musky odour was used mainly by men, who paid very dearly for it. Ambergris, a product of the sperm whale and other marine mammals, was found on the beaches or on the surface of the sea where it floated in hard, waxy lumps. Large pieces were priceless and were collectors' items. So, this magnificent specimen was lost by Jean-Louis de La Valette and was sold by Pimentel to the Republic of Venice. It had belonged to the duke for only a short time. A Médoc peasant had picked it up on the beach and had brought it to the duke as he was the head of the Maison Candale, lord of Lesparre, Bayssevelle. . .and other territories uncovered at low tide. Before gaining a reputation for the quality of its wines, Médoc had a reputation for supplying the largest quantity and the best quality of ambergris. After each storm all the locals went out in search of this precious 'animal mineral' in the same way that people nowadays look for mushrooms during the new moon.

The rights of the Admiralty of the lord of Lesparre were contested by the King himself. In 1627 a fleet of Spanish merchantmen, bringing back rare merchandise, was cast by a storm on to the shores of Montalivet, better known today for its nude bathers. In spite of all his efforts to 'save' this maritime fortune, the Duke of Epernon was obliged to bow before the majesty of Louis XIII who wanted a piece of every cake. However, his wanderings through the estate on the Médoc peninsula taught him the exact geography of his lands and their hydrographic possibilities. The following year he signed a contract with Flemish engineers to irrigate 16,320 *journaux* (that is, a little more than 550 hectares) of the marsh to the north of Lesparre. The contract provided for three years' work. In 1631 it was realized that the desired result would not be achieved. The Dutch engineers

overcame the duke's impatience and persuaded him to buy the territory of Loyrac to act as a hydraulic lock for their enterprise. In February 1633 the work of building embankments started again and the first area of reclaimed land in Médoc was created. It is called to this day the Dutch Polder.

Meanwhile, throughout this period, the Duke of Epernon governed the Guyenne with an iron rod, assisted by his son Bernard, Marquis of La Valette. His eldest son Henri, Duke of Candale, died prematurely, followed by his third son, Louis-Charles, archbishop of Toulouse. For La Valette the loss of two sons was a harsh blow and he devoted his entire attention and influence to the one remaining son, to whom he gave many gifts. Sailing close to the wind in a kingdom which was buffeted by every sort of tempest, he was feared and admired, hated

It was from this terrace, redesigned in the eighteenth century, that the Duke of Epernon, Admiral of France, supposedly watched the movements of the ships in the estuary and ordered them to lower their sails.

and adored. The Duke of Epernon was a great figure of his times and no historian of the region has been able to do him full justice. Brave under all circumstances, powerful by nature, inured to the dangers of war and to the political manoeuvres of the court, he was virtually the Regent of France under Henri III before becoming the number one suspect of Henri IV and the henchman (but not the confidant) of Louis XIII. Rigid with Gascon pride and endowed with a strong sense of personal honour, he never gave in to anyone. Indeed, on the contrary, he arrogantly demanded both the submission of his peers and a universal recognition of his qualities. It is a pity that the legend of Bayssevelle is false. If it had originated in such a person, it might well have been true.

This indefatigable traveller was always on the move, visiting every part of the kingdom and every corner of his province of Guyenne. He seldom stayed at Bordeaux or Cadillac, preferring the Château de Plassac where he was in residence from time to time; and to which he retired during his periods of disgrace. Facing Plassac is Beychevelle, and the duke must have crossed the river innumerable times in order to visit Médoc. Beychevelle was his base when he came from Blaye to make a tour of his estate of Lesparre. He may have spent a few nights at the Château Lemarque, but he was not a man often to spend more than one night in the same bed nor to watch the sails saluting him at twilight.

The Duke of Epernon was rarely sick but he always travelled with his doctor, whom he used as a companion for feasting rather than as a practising physician. In 1635, when he was 81 years of age, the duke was struck with painful and stubborn 'burning of the urine'. 'For eighteen days his malady continued and he drank nothing but ordinary water. He drank in such quantity that I do not believe any other stomach in the world would have been able to digest such an amount. He was made to sit in cold baths but all the doctor's skill was needed to cool the heated blood of this youthful nature of 84 years . . .' The chronicler made the patient three years older than he actually was, but this did not prevent the latter from reaching the age of 88 before he drew his last breath. At the time he was the most senior of the noblemen of the kingdom, having survived through the successive reigns of Henri III, Henri IV, Louis XIII and Louis XIV.

In 1643 his son Bernard took over the position of governor of Guyenne. Whereas the Duke of Epernon was not devoid of political

A century after the death of Jean-Louis de la Valette, a chronicler named Girard wrote his biography. ▶

LA VIE
DU DUC *H 8812 (1)*
D'ESPERNON,

CONTENANT

L'HISTOIRE SECRETTE
des Faits les plus mémorables arrivés
en France fous les Regnes d'Henry
III. d'Henry IV. de Loüis XIII. &
jufques fous celui de Loüis XIV. en
1642. où il eft mort.

Par M. ***.

TOME I.

A AMSTERDAM,

Chez les Janffons Van Waeefberge.
1736.

sense, his son knew only constraint and force as means of persuasion. After his father had been nominated in February 1623, he was instructed to carry out the unpleasant tasks. He already had a reputation as a despot when he succeeded to the title. 'This lord went much further than the duke his father and imagined that his sole wish should be the rule for his entire government. His pretensions went so far in this respect that he not only regarded all the people under his control as slaves but also considered that Parliament should accede to his wishes.' Under the unconditional protection of Cardinal Mazarin he committed many extortionate acts, and his reign in Guyenne was recorded as one of the most bloody periods in the entire history of Aquitaine.

Without wishing to tire even the most sympathetic reader with this list of historical facts, I would nevertheless like to dwell a little on this extraordinary person who today might be described as a paranoic fascist. His most modest title was certainly that of Baron of Bayssevelle, but it is interesting to see how an acorn can grow into an oak tree.

From 1643 onwards, the province of Guyenne was raped and pillaged by a series of taxes and forced contributions. Bernard de La Valette's father was ambitious for power and riches. His son, however, was possessed with a greed so disgusting that it defies imagination. At the time when Louis XIV, aged four years and eight months, ascended the throne of France, the Duke of Epernon, drunk with power, laid on Aquitaine a hand of steel spiced with gunpowder. Nothing was beyond his reach. An arrangement involving the sale of grain to the Spaniards, while Bordeaux was suffering a famine, alienated once and for all the good-will of the Bordeaux Parliament, of which the president was Dubernet, successor to Marc-Antoine de Gourgues. (The latter was the husband of Olive de Lestonnac, owner of Château Margaux, whose son Jean-Denis married a Pontac, another 'wine princess'.) The only title which Bernard, Duke of Epernon, lacked, was that of prince. His father had delicately proposed the elevation of Captalat de Buch into a principality but matters never progressed and he did not use the pseudo-title of Prince de Buch. However, Bernard, who wished to be addressed as Highness, tightened the regulations in order to achieve this distinction. He established, or re-established, for himself not only lordly but also sovereign rights. For example, the right of Capte, which confiscated the second-best fish in each catch; the right of Concage which claimed the tenth part of every cargo entering the harbour of Arcachon; the right of Balisage which imposed a tax of 20 *sols* on each load entering the harbour for refuge or for commerce; the right of Ancrage, of the same amount, for all ships dropping anchor along the coast; the right of Pinasse, which involved the payment of three *sols* weekly from all owners of fishing smacks. After Epernon there was a delay of one hundred years before these rights which were royal in origin were abrogated. In 1739, Louis XV obtained the verification of the maritime rights and the general commissioners of the kingdom abolished the claims of the Captaux de

Buch in 1742. The feudal spirit of Bernard de La Valette, Prince de Buch and Admiral of Médoc had made the concept of local sovereignty very durable. However, the Parliament of Bordeaux had, on several occasions, issued sweeping decrees which went so far as to involve the so-called prince with 'forfeiture and the crime of lèze-majesté'. In 1650 a decree was published, a 'decree forbidding the Duke of Epernon to take and use in future the title of noble and powerful Prince and Highness and to forbid all other persons to use them'.

The Duke of Epernon treated this condemnation with sovereign disdain and, fearing neither God nor the devil, he increased his persecution of all those who resisted him. One day he went so far as to hit the rounded stomach of the cardinal of Sourdis with his gloved hand and with his cane knocked from the cardinal's head the mitre of the archbishop of Bordeaux. For this he was excommunicated, which gave him a clear conscience to ransom, pillage, torture and kill many of the priests of the province.

Epernon's official residence was the Hôtel Puy Paulin in Bordeaux. However, as he judged this residence to be inadequate for his safety, he retired to the Château de Cadillac, from which he carried out terrifying raids on the surrounding countryside. It would appear that the Duke of Orléans, regent of the kingdom, regarded these activities with more amusement than disapproval, and the all-powerful protection of Mazarin gave La Valette scandalous impunity. Certain lords from the Guyenne region tried to form an association against him but their military inferiority prevented them from arranging a direct confrontation. So, keeping a watch on his movements, they devoted themselves to acts of counter-terrorism by attacking one or other of his estates as soon as they knew that he was more than a hundred leagues distant. Thus in 1650 they captured the château and the surrounding district of Castelnau-de-Médoc. They pillaged the region, from Lamarque to Saint-Laurent, Beychevelle and Saint-Julien, committing as many crimes in the areas belonging to the governor as the latter had permitted in their own territories. Epernon returned at a gallop. With his superior sense of psychological warfare, he let his attackers know that he was arriving. They were so afraid of him that they retreated in haste to the marsh around the Château de Blanquefort, which had been requisitioned as a matter of urgency. Thus the duke regained the advantage, almost without firing a shot. With his cavalry he then made a savage attack on Ludon, Macau, Cantenac, Margaux and Arsac, all of which he completely ravaged.

These events, on a regional level, were evidence of the excesses committed by the French nobility divided by the Fronde. The Duke of Epernon personified the power of the Regency, disgraced by the

ARREST
DE LA COVR
DE PARLEMENT
DE BOVRDEAVX.

Portant que le Roy sera tres-humblement supplié, de donner vn autre Gouuerneur à sa Prouince de Guyenne.

A BOVRDEAVX,

Par I. MONGIRON MILLANGES, Imprimeur ordinaire du Roy. 1649.

This decree from the Bordeaux Parliament, kept in the municipal library of the city, contains descriptions of the 'murders, pillage, rape and sacrilege' carried out by the Duke of Epernon.

great officers of the province. Instead of reducing this rivalry, the despotic character of La Valette only served to add fuel to the flames. In 1649, President de Pontac signed a decree of the Bordeaux Parliament petitioning the King to appoint another governor for the province of Guyenne. The citizens and members of the Fronde had to wait for a year before they received satisfaction. Meanwhile revolution broke out. The governor's impressive troops, wearing green and brown jackets, raged through the territory, particularly near Bordeaux, which they pillaged as far as the suburbs. It was a story of murder, burning, rape and sacrilege. One of the duke's lieutenants, Dudoignon, concentrated on the area of Médoc where his soldiers and sailors shipped more than 6000 *tonneaux* of wine, using Bayssevelle as a tactical base for this operation.

In 1649 the city was in a permanent state of siege, with barricades everywhere. The suburbs of Chartrons and Saint-Seurin comprised various scattered houses, surrounded by gardens, fields and vineyards which were difficult to defend. However, as far as barricades were concerned, the citizens of Bordeaux had no lack of supplies! The origin of the word barricade is *barriquade* from *barrique*, a barrel or cask. Every empty cask which could be found among the merchants, innkeepers or individual owners was requisitioned in the cause of liberty. In their revolutionary fervour, the citizens of Bordeaux found the courage to empty more than was necessary in order to strengthen their lines of defence. The two ends of the casks were removed and they were then placed vertically in serried ranks. A trench was dug in front and the casks were filled with the earth. The entire city was surrounded with them. The Princess of Condé herself with her ladies 'went to work carrying earth in small baskets, in order to encourage the other workers'. The local militia, thirsty for wine and for the blood of the duke, had to retire without the satisfaction of anything other than severe attacks of musketry fire. The city gate of Porte Dijeaux resisted every attack for twelve days.

For Bernard de La Valette, denied entry to Bordeaux by the will of the people, this was the beginning of the end.

> *A vous jouer un mauvais tour*
> *Vous vistes bien la ville preste*
> *Vous sortistes aussi sans tambour,*
> *Duc d'Epernon, et sans trompette.*

The implacable citizens took every opportunity to show their animosity towards the governor. Each morning a party of common men, and even craftsmen and middle-class citizens, went to perform their natural functions in front of the Hôtel Puy Paulin. The song-writers of the period made the most of the event.

Cette place n'est plus Ducale
Elle est de matière fécale.

This was also the time of the *Mazarinades*, satirical songs that found
their main inspiration in Bordeaux and Agen.

Mazarin en a dans le cu
Le Pernonisme est abattu;
On luy sangle les estrivières
Sur le gravier, sous les cornières:
Devant la Place du Palais
Les clers luy font un pied de nez.

An anonymous pamphlet published the 'Ironic will of the Duke of
Epernon, who is also jokingly called a prince, which his henchmen use
as a title to flatter him'. This tasteless pamphlet affected Bernard de
La Valette more than his misfortune or his disgrace. It denounced his
plebian origins – the most insufferable insult he had ever received. The
sarcasm of the period was cutting and often scatological. However it
was often witty, as can be seen from the last section of the famous will,
in which all the tradespeople who had been subjected to taxes by the
duke were invited at his death to go and dance in front of the residence
and carry flowers to his tomb in memory of his defeats.

When news came of the 'voluntary resignation' of the duke from his
position as governor, there was an explosion of joy throughout the
province. In Médoc the innkeepers put casks of wine for free con-
sumption in the village squares where the local people came to dance.
The songwriters and actors had a wonderful time trying to create the
most grotesque caricature of the duke. The climate of terror suddenly
lifted, allowing free expression and hilarity. The army, however, was
still rampaging through the countryside and the King decided to
transfer Parliament to Agen in 1652. The local inhabitants, whose city
was under the control of Anne de Maurès, the official mistress of the
Prince of Buch, was so overjoyed that they built a 'Parthenon' of four
triumphal arches, decorated with frescoes and emblems. Under one of
the arches there was a fountain of wine. Bacchus sat in state on a
barrel, holding a glass which he presented to the passers-by with these
words:

Bevons mes enfans sans soucy
Nos vignes sont en asseurance
Ceux qui les arrachoient ont perdu l'espérance
De revenir jamais icy.

The duke died in 1661 in deep disgrace. For a long time the captains of the boats who sailed up and down the estuary in front of Beychevelle saluted his disastrous memory by spitting in the water and took care not to lower their sails. I do not believe the duke ever planted a single vine. Indeed, history tells us that he tore up more than 200,000.

Two hundred years before Bernard de La Valette, Archambault de Grailly was the lord of Bayssevelle, through his mother-in-law, Assahilde de Bordeaux. The Grailly family, who were related to the Foix Candale, were the most powerful family in northern Aquitaine. A reference in the land registers of the early fourteenth century is the most ancient known to contain the name of Bayssevelle. It is found later in deeds drawn up by notaries, such as the lease contracts in which the lord of Bayssevelle allocated one of his territories to Guilhem Dupuy on 3 December 1431, or an acknowledgement signed on 3 June 1449 by Videau de Beauba in favour of the former person. From the fifteenth century onwards, evidence of the existence of the manor of Bayssevelle is well documented, but under a great variety of spellings.

Certain historians associate the legend of lowering the sails with the first English occupation. It was not a question of a naval salute, but an obligation on the part of the ships which allowed the representative of the king of England to ascertain that dues were payable. I have unfortunately been unable to find the original text giving this explanation which was very current in the early nineteenth century. There is, however, a precise explanation in all the interpretations. There was, so the story goes, a watchman who stood on a tower at the river's edge and cried *Baysse-velle!* (Lower your sails) to all the boats sailing past. Given the width of the estuary at this spot, it would have been impossible for the voice of a watchman to carry more than a tenth of the distance to the other bank (4500 metres). It is impossible to imagine a situation in which a captain, sailing upstream towards Bordeaux at a speed of about 8 knots, and taking advantage of the current in the centre of the river, would cross to the Médoc side to face both the current and the wind so as to drop his anchor and wait for the baron's henchman to arrive in a skiff to collect the dues.

Although the legend may sound very romantic, I am convinced that the true origin of the name is much more commonplace. I believe that the explanation should be sought in the roots of the language and the local geography. This is what I now propose to do, very briefly, without going to the lengths of the *encyclopédistes* of the eighteenth century who, while convinced that they were lighting candles, were in fact busy extinguishing wicks. The Gascon word for sail is *velo*. The modern transcription of this word as *voile* is perfectly orthodox. As to the first part of the name, the local Gascon word *beychet* can mean a boat or vessel of any description. It is therefore very possible that the word *Beychet-velo* simply means sailing boat.

We should, however, give some credit to the origin of the legend of lowering the sails. There must be some reason for its surviving to the

This legendary boat has sailed round the world several times . . . on wine labels.

present day. In former times the boats transporting the wine would try to get as close as possible to the estates by using the canal which flows through the territories into the estuary. However, due to the current and wind it was very often impossible to sail into the canal. Berthing would have to be completed by rowing. The name might well originate from the advice of the local workers to the sailors that they should lower their sails so that the ship could be towed into its berth.

If Beychevelle in the Middle Ages was not the busiest of ports, it was because landing there was more difficult than at Macau or Margaux, Lamarque, Pauillac or Saint-Estèphe. However, its geographical position opposite Blaye still brought in not inconsiderable trade; it was used as a port for unloading grain, cloth, stone, fish and salt, and for loading wood, rushes, game, wool and wine. It is not known when Saint-Julien and Beychevelle were founded. It can only be assumed that a Christian community was installed there on the site of a Gallo-Roman villa, as was the case at Margaux and Pauillac, and that a feudal authority, both military and fiscal, was built up. The greatest of historians have got themselves lost in the obscurantism of the high Middle Ages. Professor Charles Higounet confesses this:

Both men and events escape us totally in Bordeaux between the eighth and the tenth centuries. Narrative history, which in itself is sparse, is only concerned with invasions or certain isolated political events. The fragments of documents surviving from the ninth century are ecclesiastical charters or a few vestiges of buildings which can tell us nothing . . . navigation, both on the rivers and the sea was completely at the mercy of the Vikings from 840 onwards.

Unless there is a remarkable discovery which would reveal as much as the tombs of the Pharaohs, five hundred years of Médoc history will remain obscure. Very occasionally a parchment throws a tiny ray of light on the situation, rather like a pencil torch in a cavern. Before the thirteenth century, documents revealing any chronological coherence are very rare. The *Livre des Bouillons* kept in the municipal archives of Bordeaux starts with a list of tax exemptions granted by Jean-sans-Terre on 29 March 1205. It stipulates: *Tam in villa Burdegale quam per totam Gyrundam.* (Note that the last word should have been spelt *Gerondam*, showing how it was deformed by the Saxon accent.)

After this we find in various acts, leases, wills, contracts, deeds and other legal or clerical documents, several instances where the words *sanct. Julien* and *Bayssevelle* are mentioned. The most useful of these texts for those interested in Médoc history is without doubt the *Légende de Cénébrun*. No academic historian has been able to support the text by comparisons, as it is alone in early fourteenth-century literature as having no scientific back-up on a historical level. It is quoted from time to time almost apologetically. However, it seems to me a fascinating document and I would welcome the time to study every aspect of it in the same way that the *Chanson de Roland* was reconstituted. If I suggest that you glance through this book it is because it mentions explicitly the lordship of La Marque which controlled the parishes of Pauillac, Saint-Lambert, Saint-Julien, Sainte-Germaine (later known as Sainte-Gemme and now vanished except in the name of the Château Caronne-Sainte-Gemme), Saint-Laurent and Saint-Symphorien-de-Cussac. This covers the whole area radiating from Saint-Julien. The text gives a fascinating synopsis of about a thousand years of Médoc history. I believe that it is authentic even if contemporary copiers made it too miraculously poetic, which was very much the fashion for Christian literature of the Middle Ages when nothing could ever happen without the divine intervention of Our Lord Jesus Christ or the powerful intercession of the Blessed Virgin Mary. It appears curious to me that the saga of Cénébrun has its roots in the old Roman empire and extends into the illiterate Médoc period, with all its splendour and lack of culture.

The legend of Cénébrun begins with an astonishing mixture of Roman emperors and confused genealogies. We learn that the noble city of Bordeaux was founded by Titus and Vespasian. It is not very clear how Cénébrun, son of Vespasian, succeeded in marrying his niece Gualiène, daughter of Titus! However, Cénébrun was installed as king of Bordeaux, governing all the provinces situated on this side of the Rhône as far as the city of Arles, and from the Loire to the Pyrenees. Cénébrun built in Bordeaux the 'Pillars of Tudèle' and his wife Gualiène ordered a palace to be built which would bear her name, from which comes the name Palais Gallien (which was not built by the Emperor Gallien in the third century, as was long thought to be the case.) It was the pilgrims of St James of Compostella who maintained the legend of Galiène and her fabulous palace, which was in fact an amphitheatre. Gualiène or Galiène appears from time to time in medieval texts. As queen of Bordeaux, she became the legendary wife of Charlemagne. It is reasonably certain that a Gualiana existed in Aquitaine at the beginning of the Roman conquest. I am tempted to equate this name with that of Burdigala whose origin is still wrapped in mystery.

Cénébrun and Galiène had several children. The second son, also called Cénébrun, was the most handsome, the bravest and the strongest. His parents, especially his mother, cherished him and made him count of Médoc. They gave him all the territory as far as the ocean.

This region of Médoc was very fertile, rich in forests, water and all types of game, fish and food. Cénébrun retired to his lands with his wife Annys (Annis or Agnès?) and as his mother Galiène could not bear to be long away from him, she had a road built through the forests, on which her golden chariot carried her to the furthest reaches of Médoc. (The Roman road which crosses Médoc and of which there are still numerous traces is called the 'Lébade' or 'the road of the Queen'.) This road was built at the expense of Brunisen, a famous courtesan. In the third century, Saint Martial was bishop of Limoges. A certain Cénébrun, King of Bordeaux, and a descendant of the King described above was converted to Christianity and baptized by Saint Martial. His daughter married the Count of Limoges by whom she had one daughter called Valérie to whom the emperor of Rome (Valerian or Gallien?) gave his nephew Etienne as husband. Valérie, however, having been baptized by Saint Martial, refused to consummate the marriage. Wild with rage, Etienne had her beheaded. The executioner was struck dead and Valérie, collecting her own head, brought it to Saint Martial to have herself buried. Etienne, who was naturally astonished, promised the bishop that he would be baptized if the bishop could bring Valérie back to life. Martial said a prayer and Valérie returned to life. Etienne and five thousand of his men were baptized. Etienne was the first duke of Bordeaux.

After a lapse of time it happened that there was no legitimate heir to the duchy of Aquitaine. The Gascons chose one of the sons of the King of Castille, but he was assassinated. Then they chose a count of Poitou and through marriage the province of Guyenne passed into the family of the kings of England. There was, however, still in existence the line of the counts of Médoc. They were called alternately in each generation either Cénébrun or Ayquem-Guilhem (this name being the Gascon equivalent of Sanche-Guilhaume). They seemed to have ruled in Médoc for several centuries. One of them married the daughter of the Count of Lamarche (Lamarque) and he passed into history on a crusade against the Saracens. Having settled his affairs and entrusted his estates (including Lamarque, Castelnau, Saint-Laurent and Saint-Julien) to his brothers Ponce and Foulque, he set sail with his wife who died on the fifth day of the sea journey. Cénébrun's strength and bravery conquered the infidels although he had only a handful of Christians to face the legions of the sultan of Babylon (this was not the Babylon of Nebuchadnezzar in Mesopotamia; it was the Babylon in Egypt founded by the Greeks to the south of Cairo and was one of the first Christian bishoprics in the Orient). The sultan of Babylon arranged a truce in order to trick Cénébrun into captivity. He was successful and Cénébrun was made prisoner, although the sultan treated him like

A 300-year-old cedar tree stands in majesty over the principal courtyard of Beychevelle.   89

a king. Then, wishing to test the courage of his prisoner, he made him fight in single combat against his best knight, Enéas. Cénébrun agreed. The sultan offered him armour and the finest of his horses. Trumpets sounded and the people assembled. There were about seven thousand knights plus men and women on foot. The sultana arrived in a silver chariot, accompanied by her only daughter. There was a great silence. Enéas started to shout in order to provoke and terrify his adversary. Cénébrun kept calm and when they were first locked in battle, he succeeded in unhorsing Enéas who fell heavily to the ground. Cénébrun leapt lightly from his horse, caught Enéas by the feet and then loaded him on to his back like a pig. Bearing his burden, he remounted his steed and rode around the arena three times. Finally, to the amazement of everyone present, he deposited his enemy at the feet of the sultan. From this moment on, the sultan's daughter fell passionately in love with Cénébrun and thought only of arranging his escape.

The sultan of Babylon invited Cénébrun to embrace the beliefs and customs of the Gentiles, even though he was descended from the King of Bordeaux, son of the pagan emperor Vespasian. In return, he would receive a great number of cities in Egypt and the sultan's only daughter, Fenise, as a reward. When he heard this proposition, Cénébrun burst into floods of tears and asked if he might reflect on the proposal overnight. The Blessed Mother of Jesus Christ appeared to him during his sleep and consoled him, strengthening his faith. When he awoke, he saddened the sultan by his inflexibility. The latter, who could think of no further arguments, asked his daughter Fenise to try to persuade Cénébrun to change his mind...by words and caresses. Fenise accepted the task willingly and declared her love for the Count of Médoc. While the sultan was absent they managed to escape, taking with them a great quantity of gold and precious stones. Fenise was baptized and they took the first ship for Marseille where they arrived on the eve of 15 August. Cénébrun and his wife Fenise, who henceforth would be called Marie, bought clothing and horses and set out for Bordeaux after resting for a month. They arrived on the feast of Saint-Michel (at the time it took two weeks to travel from Marseille to Bordeaux) and on arriving, Cénébrun found that everybody, including his brothers, had believed him dead. Ponce had married the Count of Périgord's daughter and ruled over Entre-deux-Mers; while Foulque had married the daughter of the Prince of Blaye and had taken over the manor of Lamarque. On hearing this news Cénébrun concealed his fury. Leaving his wife in Bordeaux, he rode along the river bank, accompanied by his followers, and reached Lamarque and Listrac where he was refused entry. He then went to Castillon where he found the gates closed against him. Returning to Bordeaux, he recruited reinforcements and waged war with his brothers for several years. When they finally came to terms, the three brothers divided Médoc among themselves. Foulque took the manor of Lamarque with the tenure of the parishes of Pauillac, Saint-Lambert, Saint-Julien, Saint-Symphorien-de-Cussac and Saint Seurin de Lamarque. Their sister married Guichard Remond de Montaba (alias Bourg sur Dordogne). Cénébrun retired to Lesparre, a fertile spot supplied with delicious foods of all sorts. His wife bore him three sons: Guillaume, Cénébrun and Geoffroy, who became archbishop of Bordeaux and a cardinal.

The abbé Baurein was very suspicious of this text – as the story continues only up to the death of Marie – but he considers that the archbishop of Bordeaux in the year 989 was indeed a son of the lords of Lesparre. This date corresponds with the period of the first holy war which lasted throughout the second half of the tenth century and was the origin of the first Crusade, proclaimed by the pope Urban II in 1095. It should also be noted that many of the archbishops of Bordeaux had as a first name either Guillaume or Geoffroy and that the lords of Lesparre, barons of Lamarque and Saint-Julien were also called alternately Guillaume or Cénébrun.

The Château de Lamarque is one of the very rare fortified manor houses in Médoc which survived both the Hundred Years War and the Revolution. Situated between Margaux and Saint-Julien, Lamarque was a stronghold of feudal power in Médoc. Another château was built at Cussac which English mariners of the sixteenth century described as an old ruined fort. It was originally built by the *Medulli* (inhabitants of Médoc) against Julius Caesar and was called Fort César. It apparently was not far from Fort-Médoc, built by Vauban in 1689 to defend the estuary in conjunction with Fort-Paté in the middle of the river and with the citadel of Blaye.

The regions of Lamarque and Cussac do not have the benefit of a proper appellation comparable to Margaux, Saint-Julien, Pauillac or Saint-Estèphe. However, excellent wines can be found there, such as Château de Lamarque, Château du Raux, Châteaux Lanessan and Lachesnaye which are all Haut-Médoc appellations. Lachesnaye was established towards the end of the nineteenth century to replace an ancient parish already mentioned under the name of Sainte-Gemme, a contraction of Sainte-Germaine. It was closer to Beychevelle than the church of Saint-Julien but its situation opposite the *prat Lauret* did not earn it the respect of the parishioners who preferred to go to mass in a holy place further away from the witches' sabbath rites performed

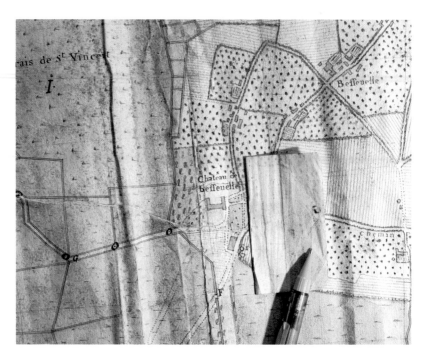

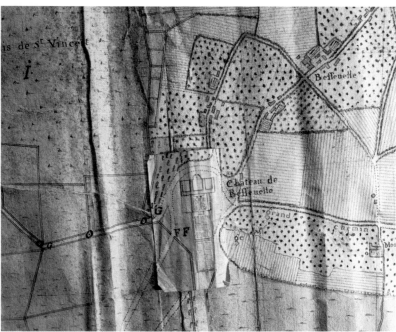

On this extraordinary document, unpublished until now, we can see the ancient boundary of the manor of Beychevelle as it existed before 1757, when M. de Brassier undertook to remodel his property and build the present château. The mapmaker of the time has attached a new design showing exactly the outline of the gardens, which were much more extensive than today. On the left side the pré Lauret *is shown. (From the collection of the Department of Archives, Bordeaux.)*

by the greatest magicians of Médoc. Even before the Revolution the parish of Sainte-Gemme was disaffected. But witchcraft continued to be practised at the *prat Lauret*. We shall make a cautious visit there.

III

It has been said that the *prat Lauret* means 'the meadow of the laurel tree'. This is incorrect. The ancient description of this place was *prat Lahouret* and the meaning of the place is very different. In Gascon the word *lahore* means 'down there far away' and *lahoùns* means 'lowest depths'. An *houral* is an evil place where unpleasant things happen. From these words we can already detect the disturbing meaning of the root *hor* or *hour*. Matters become more complicated when we see that the word *houre* is the female barn owl. In Médoc barn owls are very common, particularly in the marshes where they hunt for snakes and field mice. The local wine-producers used to nail them to the wall at the entrance of their *chais* as it was considered that owls and witches were closely related. The Gascon word *horepèt* means an old witch. So we can see that the *prat Lahouret* is a meeting place for the great witches and wizards of Médoc. They gather here under the control of the demon Léonard and dance at their sabbaths when the moon is full, while the owls hoot, frightening the wits out of passers-by.

Werewolves are wizards who, when night falls, disguise themselves as various animals (wolves, dogs, goats, piglets, asses, etc.) and roam the countryside, devouring lost children and casting evil spells over their enemies. There are also tiny witches, or fairies, who slip into the

---

◀*Odile Nomard, daughter of a wine-producer of Beychevelle, holding a mushroom weighing 2.5 kilos. (See Terroir de la Cabane in the list of wines.)*

house beneath the doors or through the key-holes. They cause terrible nightmares and bring on moon-fever. They visit young people on the eve of their wedding and make them impotent or sterile. If such a fairy takes an interest in you, it will be a scourge on your household. The fire will fail to light, the milk will turn sour, the bread will go mouldy and the wine will turn to vinegar. To find out if you are in this sort of danger, you should unsew your pillow and see if there are feathers in it arranged in a cross. If there are, you should attach pins, also in the form of a cross, to the lapel of your coat. Women should cross themselves three times and drink a bowl of fresh milk seasoned with three secret herbs which must be collected at night when there is no moon. Men should eat the heart of a young woodpecker and sew millet seed in the hem of their trousers. If you see a black chicken cross your door at twilight, this means that you are being directly threatened by a wizard. Catch the chicken in a canvas bag, wring its neck and pluck it, then cook it seven days later in new red wine. Eat it together with the family (apart from grandmother) and take care on that evening to place before your window a lighted candle in your chamberpot.

If your cow falls sick or your vines are attacked by red spiders, beetles or other parasites, this means that a wizard has put the evil eye on you. In Saint-Julien a part of the village is called *Lunègre*, which means 'the evil eye'. This bears witness to the impressive activity of some local magician. If you wish to trace the source of the problems which are affecting your property you should ask for suggestions (only one each) from those neighbours whom you trust. In this way you will be able to form an opinion and identify the magician. When you see him approach, cross the road and make a magic sign with your left hand. This means placing the thumb between the first and second fingers. Meanwhile make a secret sign of the cross with your right hand so that the magician does not see it. Then recite this spell.

Sourci té redouti
Minge merde de clouque,
Daoumán passat dibès
Que lou diable te bire la pet à l'enbès.

(Magician I fear you/Go and eat chicken dung/So that the day after next Sunday/The devil will turn your skin inside out.) As soon as you return home do not forget to turn over one of your old jackets.

Such superstitions have haunted Médoc countryfolk for centuries. I would even say that they have not yet disappeared and that Médoc is still a popular region for witchcraft. The *prat Lahouret* is a haunted area where the seven great Médoc magicians used to meet. Many stories connected with this place have virtually disappeared from popular tradition apart from a transcription made at a time when dialect was still spoken, that is, before the last war. Here is a sample which I shall translate for you.

Two hunchbacks who knew each other met one day while they were looking for mushrooms. After the normal greeting the first said to the second: 'I no longer see your hump, what have you done with it?' The second replied: 'I no longer have it because the other night when the moon was full I went to the *prat Lahouret* near the Château Beychevelle. I hid behind a thicket and waited for the seven magicians to arrive. They formed a circle in the middle of the clearing and danced while singing: 'Three times seven equals 21'...then I put myself in the middle of the circle and said: 'And one makes 22'. The magicians were very kind and allowed me to leave without my hump. That is my story. If you wish you can try it yourself.' The other hunchback waited for the next full moon and did exactly as his friend had told him. However, when the oldest of the magicians saw him he said: 'We are constantly being troubled by hunchbacks, we already have one hump and don't know what to do with it.' They then attached the first hump to the hump of the second hunchback. He returned home regretting his wasted night and the extra hump which he had acquired.

In the late sixties I took great interest in the customs, traditions and superstitions of Médoc. Having read several publications on the subject and talked with a great many local people, I wrote a series of articles and arranged a few conferences in the Bordeaux area. In 1971 I was invited to address the very respected Historical and Archaeological Society of Libourne on these matters. The newspaper *Sud-Ouest* reported the event fully, and as a result I received many letters from all parts of the province. One was from a M. and Mme D—, wine producers and vineyard owners at Y— I cannot resist quoting the following passage to you in all its spontaneity.

Monsieur, please forgive me for writing to you like this. If I understand the situation correctly, you are a person who seeks to do good. I have read about your conference concerning witchcraft. This has touched us deeply as we are the victims of such a scourge. Here in this town four houses out of seven contain people concerned with witchcraft and everything imaginable. We no longer have anyone who can carry out exorcism. We live on penicillin and the

strongest medicines. . .I therefore ask you if it would be at all possible for you to come and help us to get rid of such a burden. There
are three people in our family, including a daughter of 20 years of
age. With all our apologies. Yours sincerely.

Wine is often used in old Médoc medicinal recipes, especially for
internal use. The concoctions are sometimes very fanciful, such as one
where a local witch advises you to suck a white pebble which has been
soaked for seven days in red wine and then left for the night in the
moonlight. But we also find recipes for aromatic wines which are
similar to our vermouths and the fortified wines so popular with our
great-grandmothers. To the wine were added such items as sugar,
brandy, vanilla, cloves, orange peel, thyme, bayleaves, peach stones
and liquorice.

To combat diseases and parasites attacking the vine, remedies using
witchcraft sometimes proved powerless. Witchcraft acted principally
as a preventative measure when the vineyard was healthy. If the usual
antidotes such as chasing black chickens and traditional incantations
were not used, the following harvest was likely to be in danger. When,
due to evil fate or the negligence of the owner, it became impossible
to fight the scourge, the local priest was called in. He would walk
round the vineyard, accompanied by three choirboys with the first
carrying the cross, the second the holy water and the third the missal.
The curate recited prayers and the litanies of the saints, while scatter-
ing holy water on the branches. Each disease had its own particular
saint, but a general treatment was considered safer and all the patron
saints of the neighbouring parishes were invoked. Finally the priest
gave his blessing to the four points of the compass and enjoined the
'harmful beasts, worms and insects sent by Satan to depart immediately and retire to the depths of the forests'. Church bells were rung to
ward off storms. Several Médoc churches have, in this respect, an
excellent reputation for preventing hailstorms.

If we enter the parish of Saint-Julien from the south, that is, from
Bordeaux, we cross a bridge over the Jalle du Nord, which then continues its course along the side of the *prat Lahouret*. This bridge is
called either the Archbishop's Bridge or the Bridge of Miracles. Formerly, when the lord archbishop of Bordeaux came to confirm the
children of Saint-Julien and Beychevelle the entire population used to
gather at the bridge, which marked the parish boundary. When he
arrived, the archbishop would leave his carriage and walk slowly
across the bridge in procession, while he blessed those who had come
to greet him. It was then that miracles would happen in Saint-Julien:
the blind would regain their sight, the deaf their hearing, a hunchback

would lose his hump, an old cripple would walk again and many other supernatural events of this type would take place . . .

Evil tongues inspired by the devil deny that this legend has any foundation in truth. Others claim that the Bridge of Miracles owes its name to the remarkable change in Cussac wines, which when they were transported at night on carts from one side of the bridge to the other immediately became excellent Saint-Julien wines. I cannot decide which of these explanations to believe. Perhaps there is some truth in both of them and maybe this is why the word 'miracles' is used in the plural. Whatever the case, all this happened very long ago before the introduction of the appellations.

At the beginning of this book we noted that in 1871 local boats unloaded 2846 *tonneaux* of wine while they loaded 4207 *tonneaux*. These figures allow us to deduce that, year in year out, about 1500 *tonneaux* of *vin d'origine* was exported from Saint-Julien and Beychevelle. This quantity agrees with the statistics of communal production at the time. Why, however, was so much wine taken into Saint-Julien? There are three explanations for this. First, we must remember that the locals have always consumed a great deal of wine themselves. The wine-producers' families in an estate received a certain number of 'benefits'. They were poorly paid but had free lodging and a monthly allowance for wood, milk and wine. This custom has not entirely disappeared. As a general rule three or four litres of wine were allowed daily per man and one or two litres to the women and children. In one year a large estate would therefore absorb a considerable quantity of the local product. A separate place was reserved for this stock in the *chai*. Each day the *maître de chai* put aside a cask of ordinary wine which the workmen could use to quench their thirst, thus avoiding the use of the *grand vin*. This custom is still known today as the *piche*. I have known local workers who would drink as much as twelve litres of this wine a day. Secondly, it should be noted that the Saint-Julien commune at the end of the nineteenth century included three wholesale wine-merchants. The business was not enormous but it supplied those villages in the interior of the territory. The canton of Saint-Laurent, which numbered about 5500 inhabitants, was supplied by Saint-Julien and Beychevelle not only with wine but with several other products. There were seven shops selling 'colonial wares'. The merchants also took charge of the vinification of the harvests for small producers as some of them did not have a *chai*. They also undertook the blending which the Bordeaux shippers came to sample.

Thirdly, we should not forget the blending practised by the producers of the *grands crus*. In order to correct a lack of colour and body in the wine, especially after cold and damp harvests, wine strong in alcohol and rich in colour was imported from Spain or from the Côtes du Rhône to act as a 'booster'. Professor René Pijassou has made a careful study of these practices which were called 'working in the English way'. I must stress that it was concern for improvement which was the motivation of the vineyard owners. At the time there was no question of fraud, but of a 'loyal and constant' practice to improve the wine's quality while supporting its extreme delicacy with a proportion of more robust wine. Very often the addition was made by topping up the cask. In this way the *cru* wine received progressively an addition of 'booster' wine during the three, four or five years it was maturing, which corresponded to the natural evaporation of the wine in the cask. In general the 'topping up' of the wine in the *chai* was done in a traditional way. Henri Martin, who has experienced 80 vintages, remembers clearly the casks of Spanish wine being unloaded on the quay at Saint-Julien. And I well remember a paragraph from one of the early Michelin guides for Spain written in the thirties: 'Rioja wines

Each great cru *has its collection of vintages in which all the harvests over more than a century are represented. At Ducru-Beaucaillou 'volume one' of the library goes back to 1860.* ▶

are very much in demand for adding to the Bordeaux *crus*.' I would point out, however, that Rioja wines have never been topped up with Médoc *crus*.

Until it became the habit to bottle wines at the château a few years ago, the estate charged the merchants 'storage and maturing costs' which amounted to 0.75 per cent per month and 3 per cent *collage*. In the nineteenth century the Médoc wines were kept in casks for ten years. I have a document written by a shipper in 1820 which offers the *cru* of 'Saint-Julien Galant Médoc of 1811 at 450 francs the cask or 2.50 francs the bottle. The same wine in 1815 cost 350 francs the cask and 2 francs the bottle.' The document continues: 'We cannot consider the four preceding years as two are mediocre, that is 1816 and 1817, and the last two, 1818 and 1819, are too new for drinking. We need to wait another two or three years before bottling them and at this stage the customer would be unwise to buy them.'

The Château Beychevelle label bears an illustration of a ship lowering its sail. This craft has sailed round the world several thousand times. It is one of the most famous labels in Bordeaux, and its present design probably dates from the beginning of the century. Of all the labels from Saint-Julien and Beychevelle the oldest is that of Ducru-Beaucaillou which with its simple typography well illustrates the art of *vignette* in the second half of the nineteenth century. Such illustrations began to appear in Bordeaux in 1817 when the first lithographic press was installed by a local architect called Cabillet. This was the result of an invention by Aloys Senefelder, developed in Paris in 1814 by Baron Charles de Lasteyrie. The first real lithograph printer was

▲ *A handwritten notice from a Bordeaux wine-shipper in 1820.*

On this old label from Ducru-Beaucaillou the château is not mentioned. Nevertheless, the illustration of the château takes up most of the space on the label. ▶

Gaulon, a Créole by origin who was a 'professor of writing'. Fascinated by the new technique developed by Cabillet in Bordeaux, the professor established himself in 1920 in the rue Saint-Rémi. From 1827 onwards lithography became very popular, and the humorous painter Gustave de Galard worked actively with Gaulon, as we know from Goya's illustrations. The first wine labels were lithographed on the Gaulon press. The name of the *cru* and the year were usually shown, together with an illustration or a coat of arms; sometimes there was also the name of the owner and of the commune producing the wine. On Gaulon's death in 1858, his wife continued the business and sixteen years later handed it over to her son-in-law, Michel Wetterwald, whose descendants are still printers in Bordeaux.

At that time it was very rare for wine to be bottled at the estate. During the ten-year maturing period in cask, the owners had to resign themselves to buying bottles which were very costly in order to keep the unsold quantities of their harvests which they might be left with. They kept for their own use a small quantity of the best vintages in bottles. The shippers themselves usually dispatched wine in casks. We know that the importers and local retailers where the wine was to be consumed arranged the bottling themselves, often on their customers' premises. In order to ensure the authenticity of the wine they ordered bundles of labels printed in Bordeaux, but some of them had their own personalized labels showing their brand name. (A certain Duke of Morny had labels printed with his own monogram in order to build up his collection of great wines.) At this period business in Bordeaux was flourishing. The great merchant houses arranged the wine trade among themselves and argued about the allocation of the best *crus*. These were loaded in thousands of *tonneaux* on armed ships at Bordeaux or Nantes which may well have come from the five continents.

In Médoc the idea of a *cru* as we understand it today really started after the official classification of 1855. The shipper Lawton wrote in his journal with regard to Saint-Julien:

> This parish, which is fine and productive, can be considered among the best of Médoc ... in fact its ordinary wines could be classified as fine wines. The body of the wine is generally soft and it has the advantage over the other Médoc fine wines in that it has something extra which is smooth and mellow. In addition it has a good colour, consistency, charm and distinguished vigour. All its wines are very suitable for England.

The English were in fact the very best customers for clarets, in particular for Graves wines, a generic term including all the *crus* planted on the stony slopes or plateaux of the left bank.

It was at this time that William Franck, the first author of the *Treatise on the Wines of Médoc* described the wines of Saint-Julien.

> The wines produced by this commune can be compared in quality to those of Margaux and Cantenac. They have, however, a particular bouquet which clearly distinguishes them from the other Médoc communes. They have a better colour and more flavour than Pauillac wines and need a further year to achieve maturity. They need to be stored for five or six years in cask and they then combine all the best qualities characteristic of first-class wines.

A century later one of the most respected English writers on wine, Edmund Penning-Rowsell, disagreed with Franck and stated that the wines of Saint-Julien were 'less full-bodied and powerful than the Pauillac wines. They combine fruitiness and delicacy and develop a splendid bouquet when they are fully mature.' Personally, I agree with this statement. In general the wines of Saint-Julien are less robust than those from Pauillac and Saint-Estèphe. Like the wines from Margaux they are rather sensitive to cold years (although Ducru-Beaucaillou seems to me to be particularly resistant). Logically, because of their geographical situation, the three Léoville wines are closer to those from south Pauillac. Las Cases, which nowadays claims to be the best of the three, can still surprise you with its lack of consistency; but in certain years it can be of exceptional quality, comparable to *1e cru* wines. Penning-Rowsell protests strongly in his text at the 'the enormous, hideous bottle which is placed on a prominent bend in the road as a means of attracting disagreeable publicity for the products of Saint-Julien.' Henri Martin, although he has been photographed in front of this monstrosity, also criticizes its position at the entrance to the charming village of Beychevelle, exactly opposite the gates of Château Gloria. This monument to bad taste was made in the thirties for an extravagant Festival of Wine in Bordeaux. A local association, La Grappe Beychevelloise, had worked night and day to set up the monstrosity. After the festival, under the direction of Désiré Cordier, it was decided to make the bottle a permanent fixture. The town council exchanged land with Colonel Kappelhoff, owner of Château Saint-Pierre, to change the bend in the road so that the bottle could be placed there. Henri Martin did not approve of it but gave way to a majority vote.

In the fifties, another Festival of Wine took place at Pauillac. All the major Bordeaux shippers dressed in turn of the century costumes and the ladies from the various châteaux (the Rothschild, the Cruse, the Charmolüe, etc.) were charmingly dressed in Médoc peasant costume. Henri Martin took the part of Paulin Desquet. The entire festival was successful and in very good taste. The bottle in question was skilfully transported to Pauillac and after the celebrations it was stored in a barn where Henri Martin hoped it would stay. Public opinion, however, would not allow this and the mayor was obliged to reinstate it.

The bottle, which is like a small water-tower, acts as an orientation mark for light aircraft flying over Médoc. It was recognized on 14 October 1978 by Robert Wagner who was taking the former minister of communications, Aymar Achille-Fould, Emile Simon, director-general of the Post Office and Marcel Nodiot, at that time deputy mayor of Villacoublay on a trip. Their aircraft landed on the football ground of Saint-Julien-Beychevelle to commemorate the first airmail postal link. This had happened on 15 October 1913, when Lieutenant Ronin, flying a 60-horsepower Morane and Saulnier monoplane, linked Villacoublay with Saint-Julien, carrying a sack of mail weighing 10.6 kilos. The mailbag contained letters intended for the West Indies. It was delivered to the captain of the ship *Le Pérou* which was sailing from Pauillac for Pointe-à-Pitre. This service meant a saving of fourteen days over the traditional postal service. At that time the landing

---

Like an obelisk, the famous bottle of Saint-Julien-Beychevelle raises its neck towards the skies.

field was a field of luzern-grass belonging to the Château Léoville-Barton.

François Mauriac did not like the Bordeaux people but he did like their wine. Though not a great drinker he was a connoisseur of fine wines. One sip was enough to set his intellectual processes in motion. In this respect it would seem to me that Saint-Julien wines are not the best for sporting types. As with all major works of art, these wines create an impression by their purity and the genius involved in their production, which Mauriac called 'skill'. In order to make my meaning clearer let me quote the words of the master: 'It is a wine which is difficult to understand as it is so lacking in contrivance.' Furthermore, he added: 'It is not that Bordeaux wine is not as lively as Burgundy wine. But there is nothing to approach the finesse of the wines from Haut-Brion, Gruaud-Larose, Margaux or Lafite.'

If, long before Mauriac, Pascal had wished to pinpoint this spirit of finesse, I am convinced that he would have chosen as an example the wines of Saint-Julien.

The *Crus*

The term '*cru classé*' is used only in describing the *crus* which were part of the official 1855 classification. This date is not repeated each time the classification is mentioned.

 The number of coloured glasses beside the name gives an idea of the quality of the wine in relation to its selling price. This measurement, which has been made objectively, is naturally subject to fluctuation. It should be taken as a rough guide to the quality rather than constituting a formal classification.

Certain varieties use one or more secondary labels to denote the second product of their property. These 'second varieties', which are mentioned in this list, are followed by an arrow which indicates the main variety.

This symbol shows that a particular variety is a second product of a larger property.

Beauregard (Château)

→ Capdelong

Beychevelle (Château)

Commune: Saint-Julien-Beychevelle **Owner:** Société civile du Château Beychevelle-Achille-Fould **Director:** Aymar Achille-Fould **Manager:** Maurice Ruelle **Maître de chai:** Lucien Soussotte **Chef de culture:** Guy Bougnaud **Surface area of vineyard:** 72 hectares (total property 250 hectares) **Average age of vines:** 20 years **Grape production:** 60% Cabernet-Sauvignon, 28% Merlot, 8% Cabernet-Franc, 4% Petit-Verdot **Production:** 250,000–300,000 bottles **Local sales:** Tel (56) 59 23 00, **and by direct mail:** Château Beychevelle, 33250 Saint-Julien-Beychevelle **Retail sales:** 20–25 firms

4ᵉ cru classé

In 1866 the Societé d'Agriculture de la Gironde awarded the gold medal for the most outstanding vineyard to François Guestier. That year the Guestier family were obliged to sell their property, Château Batailley in Pauillac, in order to pay inheritance taxes. However, they kept Beychevelle, whose magnificent reputation suited their standing as local wine-producers. Eight years later, the Parisian banker Armand Heine bought it for 1,600,000 gold francs and bequeathed it to his daughter Marie-Louise, who married Charles-Achille Fould. He thus inherited Beychevelle by marriage and added a political element by way of his family: his grandfather Achille Marcus had been the Minister of State for Napoléon III and his father had been a member of parliament. His son Armand was Minister of Agriculture and his grandson Aymar, who is still at the height of his career, has had the responsibility of various ministerial functions in the governments after de Gaulle. It is curious to note that in each century since the Middle Ages the estate of Beychevelle has belonged to powerful men, be they appointed by royal, imperial or republican governments.

As far back as it is possible to trace in the history of Médoc, the barony of Beychevelle has been in the patrimony of the Grailly-Foix Candale family, a very powerful dynasty from Aquitaine. In the first part of this book we have seen how Jean-Louis Nogaret de La Valette, first Duke of Epernon, married the last heiress of the Foix-Candale who owned the lordship of Lamarque, which included Beychevelle, Saint-Lambert and Saint-Laurent, attached to the estate of Lesparre. After the death of Bernard de La Valette, the second Duke of Epernon, these estates were confiscated by the Royal Treasury as payment for the family's colossal debts. In the late 1660s the manor of Lamarque was decimated. The territory of Beychevelle was itself divided into several parts and it was at this period that those lands which should have become Ducru-Beaucaillou and Branaire were detached from the principal estate. Even today these two properties still give the impression of being enclaves. In 1674, after many complicated and convoluted transactions, the Duke of Rendan purchased what remained of Beychevelle from the French Crown. It would seem that almost a century before the great Médoc châteaux became famous, the production from the *cru de Rendan* was very well known. At this period, the vineyards of Médoc had been developed only to a small extent. Issan, under the name of Théobon, and Margaux, 111

The façade and gardens of Beychevelle, seen from the river.

under the name of La Mothe, were the most famous *crus* of south Médoc. To the north was Lamarque (completely ignored in the classification of 1855 due to a lack of production in the preceding century), then Beychevelle, Latour, Lafite and Calon. In the 1855 classification the only ones to be given the distinction of 'château' were Lafite, Margaux, Latour, Issan and Beychevelle. The Duke of Rendan kept the property of Beychevelle for eighteen years before selling it to President d'Abadie, the head of a famous legal family in the Bordeaux Parliament which was related to the best middle-class and merchant families of the town.

Many writers maintain that the d'Abadie family neglected the vineyards of Beychevelle. This seems to me to be a rather harsh condemnation, especially if we consider that the vine only started to flourish on the pebbly slopes of Médoc in the

second half of the eighteenth century. In his book on Médoc, M. René Pijassou writes: 'The genius of the Bordeaux aristocrats in creating the great red wines of Médoc was more or less unnoticed by their contemporaries both in the provincial capital of Aquitaine and in Parisian society.' However, a little later in the same work he quotes Professor Enjalbert: 'The Bordeaux notables at the beginning of the eighteenth century took care to serve their guests with fine wines; château wines which were gathered on private estates; wines which were aged in cask and then bottled locally.' Although it would appear correct that Parisian society was not familiar with the new French clarets, this *vin de grave* played an integral part in Bordeaux life.

It is not known exactly when the Beychevelle estate was transferred to the *sieur de Brassier*, a counsellor at the Bordeaux Parliament. It must have been between 1730 and

Watercolour showing the view from the terrace towards the estuary.

1740. The Marquis François-Etienne de Brassier had, at the beginning of the eighteenth century, united a certain number of the estates which had formerly belonged to the Foix-Candale. These were Lamarque, Poujaux à Moulis and Beychevelle, plus isolated parcels of land at Saint-Laurent. In 1740 he gathered 80 *tonneaux* of *grand vin*: a very large quantity for the period. Oxen and horses were used for the ploughing. The vat-house had three presses and 13 large vats. The top-quality wines were stored in new casks each year, showing that no expense was spared to maintain quality. Prices were fixed according to the vintage, from 250 to 600 pounds for a *tonneau*, which was an average price for the *3ᵉ crus*. Brassier appears as a rival to the contemporary *seigneurs des vignes* and competed in high living with other grand families such as Ségur, Rauzan, Pichon-Longueville, Gasq, Gorce and so on. He built the present château in 1757, using materials from the medieval manor dating from the time of the Foix-Candale. It is a rare and outstanding example of architecture from the transitional period between the styles of Louis XIV and Louis XV. Professor F.-G. Pariset gives us this short description of the building:

> The façades are decorated with balustrades and urns and the bays of the grand floor of the main courtyard are decorated with metal bars. On the other side, the façade is almost identical and the terrace leads to a park in the French style which descends to the river. The general effect is grandiose and pleasing. The central part of the front entrance is dominated by a pediment, the supports of which are made up of twisted columns ascending towards a shield at the point of the triangle. The sinuous design of the columns and the urns would be inconceivable in the Ile-de-France. The same motifs are found on doorways or façades throughout the region and this joyful exuberant fantasy is typical of the vitality found in baroque design . . .

Brassier, who was a perfectionist in everything, designed the port of Beychevelle in an ultra-modern way for the period. Consequently he had an almost complete monopoly on the merchandise intended for the neighbourhood and the estates up-country. He was able to impose a tax on these goods which brought in a substantial supplementary income. In the heyday of the Château, guests who disembarked at the steps leading up to it would exclaim with admiration on seeing this opulent site, and were overwhelmed when they walked through the gardens designed in the style of Le Nôtre.

M. Aymar Achille-Fould tasting his wine under the gaze of the Duke of Epernon.

Even nowadays, the parterres at Beychevelle, the banks of flowers on the riverside terraces and the massive imposing building itself are worthy of Versailles. In their own way they have helped the fame of the *cru*, since they have been described in numerous papers and magazines throughout the world. Three gardeners, the chief of whom is Robert Bertin, are now employed all the year round to maintain the gardens. The flowers, which are cultivated in greenhouses, are transplanted to the beds according to the season, and the annual garden budget for Beychevelle is approximately 350,000 francs. I could not possibly speak of the plants around the château without mentioning the cedar of Lebanon which has been standing for two centuries in the centre of the principal courtyard. There is also a superb 300-year-old evergreen oak in the adjacent farm.

After his father's death, François. Arnaud de Brassier guided the family fortunes successfully until the Revolution, when his château was taken over by the local 115 peasants. Local legend has it that, while attempting to escape, he was hunted like a wild animal. A little later he challenged an adversary to a duel because of an affair of honour and killed his opponent. He then went into exile and was lost in history. When his mother died the family property would have been taken over by the nation but for the fighting nature of his sister, Mme de Saint-Hérem, who succeeded in winning everything back and then selling it to Jacques Conte, a Bordeaux ship-owner who was also in private business. At the very beginning of the nineteenth century, Conte chartered pirate craft which succeeded in seizing the cargoes of ships sailing near the mouth of the estuary at Bordeaux. It was a new way of interpreting the legend of 'lower your sails'. These maritime exploits did nothing to improve the reputation of the *cru*, which had gone into decline when Conte sold it in 1825 to his nephew Pierre-François Guestier, son of Daniel, and an associate of Hugh Barton (see Langoa). The new owner was very keen on horses and founded the 'Guestier stables' which led him to build the south wing of the farm where, according to Clive Coates, he bred generations of thoroughbreds from a splendid English stallion called Young Governor. To continue in the tradition of the Beychevelle owners, he was elected to the Chamber of Deputies in Bordeaux. In 1855 Beychevelle was put at the bottom of the *crus classés* of Saint-Julien, with the *4ᵉ crus*, behind Saint-Pierre, Talbot and Branaire. During the thirty years when the château was owned by Jacques Conte its reputation had certainly suffered. Being unable to obtain official quotations during this period, the Bordeaux shippers, who were commissioned by the Chamber of Commerce to prepare a basis for the classification, were unable to give a better position to Beychevelle.

After the Guestier family the house of Fould brought to the estate the power of their finance and the constancy of their care. Armand Achille-Fould, former Grand Master of the Commanderie du Bontemps, was a conscientious owner and an ardent exponent of public relations. Helped by the charm and discretion of his second wife Elizabeth (better known as Lileth), he gave to Beychevelle his generous warmth and brought world-wide fame to its label.

Strengthened by its new administration and with outside capital helping the family (Aymar, Etienne, Marie-Geneviève, son and daughter of Armand), the property is now managed by a committee. Chaired by Aymar Achille-Fould, the committee consists of members of the family and representatives from the Garantie Mutuelle des Fonctionnaires and other smaller shareholders. Beychevelle seems to have moved with the times and has taken on a new lease of life.

Today Château Beychevelle is listed as a *2ᵉ cru*. Its promotion was due to the intelligent work carried out by a small group of men under the leadership of the Achille-Fould family. Pierre Hazera and Robert Raymond, who are the *maîtres de chai*, Henri Laboual, *chef de culture*, and Gabriel Frette, head gardener, have been the remarkable craftsmen who have implemented the successful change. Maurice Ruelle is the manager of the company and is one of the best wine-producers in the Bordeaux region. He has also had the invaluable assistance of Lucien Soussotte in the *chai*, Guy Bougnaud in the vineyard and Robert Bertin in the gardens. For the last ten years or so, Beychevelle has been successful with most of its vintages. If the 1960s decade does not appear to be very favourable, the 1970s have supplied us with wines which are constantly improving. From 1980 onwards they have been superb. I offer a toast to Beychevelle and lower my voice as a sign of respect.

Branaire (Château)

4ᵉ cru classé

Commune: Saint-Julien-Beychevelle **Owner:** SA du Château Branaire-Ducru **President:** Nicolas Tari **Managing director:** Jean-Michel Tapie **Chef de culture:** Joseph Berrouet **Maître de chai:** Marcel Renon **Surface area of vineyard:** 48 hectares (total property 100 hectares) **Average age of vines:** 18 years **Production:** 250,000–300,000 bottles **Local sales:** Tel (56) 59 25 86, **and by direct mail:** SA du Château Branaire-Ducru, 33250 Saint-Julien-Beychevelle **Retail sales:** Traditional Bordeaux outlets

---

Braneyre was one of the areas detached from the estate of Bernard de La Valette, Duke of Epernon when, after his death in 1666, his property was taken by the French Crown to pay off his debts. More or less at the same time that the Duke of Rendan purchased Beychevelle, a certain M. Du Luc became owner of Branaire. Beychevelle and Branaire are the two proud sentinels of the Saint-Julien appellation which greet you at the entrance to the territory as you come from Bordeaux, one to the right and one to the left of the road. Although not competing with the magnificence of its opposite neighbour, Château Branaire nevertheless offers to the visitor a fine building in the directoire style, elegant and restrained in its proportions and surrounded by outbuildings and *chais* which are discreetly arranged. When we enter the complex of buildings we find a late-eighteenth-century orangery which is a gem of aristocratic simplicity.

The Du Luc family seem to have emerged almost unscathed from the Revolution. For almost two centuries the *cru* has maintained a good reputation and this earned it a classification in 1855 as a *4ᵉ cru*. After the death of Louis Du Luc in about 1860, his son Léo sold the property to one of his cousins, Gustave Ducru, at a time when the latter had just been cut off from parts of the Ducru-Beaucaillou inheritance by his sister Mme Ravez. In order to give his wine a brand name, Gustave Ducru re-established the place-name of Branaire to which he added the two family names of Duluc and Ducru. (For a century now the brand is best known as Branaire-Ducru.) He died without direct descendants in 1879 and his two nephews were the heirs: the Court of Ravez recently ennobled by Charles X, and the Marquis of Carbonnier de Marsac, who shortly afterwards transferred the estate to two distant cousins, Viscount Périer de Larsan and Court Jacques de La Tour. Their coronets still decorate the four corners of the Château Branaire label as if they had been forgotten and left behind in the cloakroom. Following them the estate was bought by a Lyons industrialist in 1922 who wanted to place his capital in a second residence. M. Mital, founder of his own business, pioneer of new techniques, with a curious and inventive personality notable for the development of rice-growing in the Camargue, did not take a direct interest in his Médoc château. Branaire suffered from the absence of a master and was in a state of deep depression when Jean Tapie, who had just returned from Algeria, saved it from oblivion. Like his son-in-law Nicolas Tari at Giscours, Jean Tapie undertook the renovation of the vineyards and the restoration of the *chais*. In ten years, from 1952 to 1961, he restored Château Branaire to health. Its self-confidence returned and the careful work produced results. He effected a resurrection, as Branaire, from the sixties onwards produced a succession of astonishingly good vintages.

The very modest reputation of Branaire over half a century inspired an English novelist (whose name I have unfortunately forgotten) to write a charming novel, of which the pilot is as follows. One evening the rich squire of a small country town was entertaining to dinner one of his friends who was fat, old and unattractive, but who 117

The façade of Château Branaire.

had a cultivated wit and prided himself on possessing the best palate of his generation. His host served at table a wine which had been decanted and challenged his guest to identify it. The latter took up the challenge and asked what the stake would be. His host replied: 'Anything you care to mention, my friend. Anything you care to mention.' The fine wine-taster replied: 'Well, if I win, you shall grant me the hand of your daughter.' The young lady of the house blushed deeply when she heard these words and did not appreciate the joke at all, but her father burst out laughing and said: 'Agreed.' His wife interrupted to remonstrate gently with her husband for getting so carried away with

M. Marcel Renon, maître de chai *at Branaire*.

the wager. He replied: 'My dear, there is no question of a wager, it is merely a farce. The wine in this carafe comes from a small estate of which there are thousands in France. Our friend has absolutely no chance of identifying its exact origin or its date. I have just received the wine, which never before has been in my cellar, which is one of the best in the county. You really shouldn't take the claims of this old fellow seriously!' His wife gazed at her daughter, who at the age of 22 was considered a very good catch. She was beautiful, young and rich and there was no lack of suitors among well-born and handsome young men. Her glance then turned towards the wine expert who was seated at her side and she replied to her husband: 'Of course, my dear. But even if there was only one chance in a thousand it would still be too much!' Her husband, without losing his good humour, replied: 'No, no, I promise you there is not the least chance. Let him make a fool of himself.' No one said anything further. The cherubs which were flying above the chandelier in the dining room looked like large bats. The guest took his glass between his thumb and his first finger. He gazed at it thoughtfully before turning it clockwise and plunging his large, ugly nose inside the crystal goblet. With his eyes closed, he took a sip between his thick lips and then ran it around his mouth for what seemed like several centuries. Finally he replaced his glass with a preoccupied air and launched into a scientific analysis of which I shall spare you the details. In general his comments were: 'This wine is not this or that, it is more like this one or that one. It has not been produced under these or those conditions and it would be more in the style of —— but not of the type —— or perhaps this *cru* is ——' In short he indulged in a sort of vivisection like a commentary made by a master of wine. Finally, when the situation was becoming unbearable for his hosts, he announced: 'Château Branaire, 1904.' His host grew pale, and when his wife saw this she started to tremble and the chain reaction terminated with a sob from the young lady who hurriedly left her place. In an oily yet modest way, the hero of the evening turned short-sightedly towards his host and said: 'Now my very dear friend, what do you say of our bet?' His dear friend had nothing at all to say and his wife considered it was time to leave the table. At this precise moment, the maid appeared in the dining room and, addressing the guest, showing him what she held in her hand, said: 'Sir, I believe you have left your spectacles in the office!'

Branaire is a distinguished wine. Its distinction is original and personal, if somewhat unconventional. How can I explain this? If, for example, you are looking at a line of high fashion models, you will first see them as a total entity. But one of these marvellous creatures will have something extra ... and this small extra quality will single her out and attract your attention. Branaire possesses this extra charm which gives it an exciting quality. Certainly it has noble origins, but that is not enough to describe it adequately. Perhaps we should say that Branaire is a warm and communicative wine. There are extraordinary overtones of fruitiness, combined with a persistent aftertaste of new oak. (The château renews its supply of casks by 50 per cent every year.) It is surprising to be able to taste this in new wines, as with Beaujolais. Branaire is a wickedly seductive wine which has left me with the memory of strange emotions. Is it because of the territory, the microclimate, the quality of the grapes, the way the vines are treated or the methods used in harvesting? I believe that to a large extent the method of wine production used by Marcel Renon and the finest quality casks are responsible for its individual personality. We can put what we like in writing but in a blind tasting Branaire always stands out, whether we like it or not. I will tell you a secret: I love Branaire.

Bruyères (Domaine des)

cru artisan

Commune: Saint-Julien-Beychevelle **Owner:** Lucien Moreau **Surface area of vineyard:** 340 square metres **Average age of vines:** 10 years **Grape production:** 2/3 Cabernet-Franc, 1/3 Merlot **Production:** Approximately 2000 bottles **Local sales and direct mail:** Domaine des Bruyères, 33250 Saint-Julien-Beychevelle

When someone has started to work at 14½ years of age in a merchant's *chai* at Pauillac and has been an apprentice there for 5 years; when he has worked at Château Latour for 11 years and subsequently has been for 28 years the *maître de chai* and Château Gruaud-Larose, then he knows exactly what he is talking about with regard to wine. Lucien Moreau is a descendant of the Billa family which has been known for centuries in Saint-Julien, and it is here that he has the small *chai* which houses the wine of the Domaine des Bruyères. This third of a hectare of land belongs to the family and was used for subsistence. It supplied a little maize for the chickens, some cabbages, potatoes, beets and a little corn. Then it was planted with Luzern-grass and, ten years ago, Lucien Moreau planted it with vines, having discussed the project with Georges Pauli, director of the Domaines Cordier. The parcel of land, which had been cultivated for fodder and grain for almost fifty years, proved to be excellent territory. Its yield is very satisfactory as it produces between six and seven casks of wine each year. The quality is remarkably good if we bear in mind the relative youth of the plants. Curiously enough, there is no Cabernet-Sauvignon; with Lacoufourque, it is the only vineyard in Saint-Julien (and probably one of the very rare vineyards in Médoc) which uses for most of its base Cabernet-Franc grapes.

Lucien Moreau is considering retirement in the not too distant future and he hopes that one or the other of his two sons-in-law will take up the torch and continue to work the Domaine des Bruyères. When this little property was inherited the deeds were finalized by exchange, without using the services of a lawyer. In order to regularize the situation, a public notarized deed had to be issued, with two witnesses. I personally wish to witness publicly that Lucien Moreau makes a good wine.

Caillou Blanc (du Château Talbot)

Commune: Saint-Julien-Beychevelle **Owner:** See Château Talbot **Surface area of vineyard:** 5 hectares **Average age of vines:** 10 years **Grape production:** 100% Sauvignon **production:** 50,000 bottles **Retail sales:** Exclusively from Maison Cordier

This is the only white wine from Saint-Julien and like the Pavillon Blanc of Château Margaux it may be considered a curious exception. It should be noted in passing that several *crus classés* of Médoc produced a small quantity of white grapes in the eighteenth and nineteenth centuries which were principally intended for the personal use of the owners. Until the thirties, Château Lagrange also had a considerable quantity of white grapes. The vineyard of Caillou Blanc de Talbot is situated in the centre of the AOC Saint-Julien area which in its way is a sort of luxury.

The wine is usually very fresh and fruity. I consider it to be one of the very best white Bordeaux wines.

Capdelong (Château)

Commune: Saint-Julien-Beychevelle **Owner:** Henri Palomo **Surface area of vineyard:** 4 hectares plus 2.5 hectares on lease (Moulin de la Bridane), all situated between Talbot and les Léoville **Average age of vines:** 40 years **Grape production:** 2/3 Cabernet, 1/3 Merlot **Production:** Approximately 10,000 bottles **Local sales:** Tel (56) 59 00 74, **and by direct mail:** Château Candelong, 33250 Saint-Julien-Beychevelle **Retail sales:** In particular, Maison Barrière Frères in Bordeaux

cru grand artisan

'I do not believe in producing wine sitting behind my desk,' states Henri Palomo, better known locally by his nickname of Riquet. When the weather is fine, Palomo can be seen in his vineyard, and when it is raining he is in his *chai*. His days are always very busy. Can you imagine the work involved if you cultivate, on your own, more than six hectares of first-class vines on Médoc territory, then produce the wine and bottle it? 'Formerly we gathered in the harvest and shortly afterwards sold the wine,' he says. 'Now we have to keep it until we bottle it!' Apart from the harvest, when outside workers are hired, Henri Palomo really does carry out all the work himself with only the help of his modest but energetic wife Claire. The property was established by Robert Thibaut, Claire Palomo's father, and his father, Paul Thibaut, was in charge of the vines at Léoville-Poyferré. The property was originally a life purchase of 500 square metres. Subsequently Henri Palomo bought 9000 *pieds* of vines (about one hectare) from one Hugon. In 1974, at the time of the Thibaut succession, 2½ hectares retured to his wife. Furthermore, a similar surface area was leased to the brand of Château Moulin de La Bridane. This label suits his production as well as the label of Château Capdelong. 'It is strange,' says Henri Palomo, 'as it is the same wine, yet customers who know their wines prefer Bridane to Capdelong or vice versa. They claim that the former has this quality or the latter has that quality.' The Château Capdelong brand is recently founded.

M. Henri Palomo on his property.

Up until 1946, the Palomo production bore the label of Château Beauregard. But the Clauzel family who owned the Château Beauregard at Pomerol started legal proceedings against him. In the first instance Henri Palomo won the case at Libourne, but when it went to appeal at Bordeaux he lost it. He stopped the litigation and chose another name based on the land register deeds of his property. The most embarrassed in this affair was the Maison Barrière, wine merchants in Bordeaux who had built up a loyal following for the brand of Beauregard in Saint-Julien. For Henri Palomo it was not really a great drama and, as his wine was just as good as previously, he continued to sell it very successfully. In order to diversify his production commercially he has just registered a new brand, called Château Cam du Long, another area of his property. This name is certainly very ancient. It means 'the path of the Long'. The Long is the small stream which drains the water from the Talbot plateau and which has given its name to Château Langoa.

Henri Palomo is not a person to let the grass grow under his feet. He is much respected locally. Pruning the vines is a full-time job for him and he works at it almost continuously from early November until the end of March, except when frost or bad weather prevent him from doing so. I would be curious to know exactly how many times he has opened and shut his secateurs . . . a very modest estimation would be that during the last ten years he has clipped about 600,000 shoots. What more need be said?

As his name indicates, Henri Palomo is of Spanish origin. His parents arrived in Cussac in 1921 where his father became gardener at the Château Lachesnaye. They became French citizens before the war. Henri was born at Cussac and he is a fully-fledged inhabitant of Médoc. He has a small stone house on the edge of Saint-Julien, on the left as you go towards Pauillac. On the other side of the road is the boundary of Léoville-Las Cases. The shutters are painted light blue and three rose bushes (which I have not included in my estimation for the secateurs) stand guard along the fence. There is no name over the door, nor any alluring placard to tempt a possible customer. However, by word of mouth alone, Henri Palomo succeeds in selling about 12,000 bottles of his wine to casual customers. At weekends during the season, tourists stop in the village square and ask where they can buy wine. M. Palomo is not to be found in his vineyard on Sundays, but it is highly probable that he will be in one of his two *chais*, looking after his latest harvest. I know of no owner who is more demanding of himself.

There is a shortage of space in which casks can mature, so the larger part of his wines are bottled from vats stored elsewhere. It must be admitted that the result is very good, but what would it be if each of his harvests could be stored in his own vats? To ensure high quality the wine is lightly filtered when it is bottled. Half of each vintage is kept for M. Palomo's personal customers. The other half is sold to the wine trade in Bordeaux, such as the faithful Maison Barrière. Unfortunately it is no longer possible to find a wine-producer like Henri Palomo in Saint-Julien. ·

Capdet (Château)

cru artisan

Commune: Saint-Julien-Beychevelle **Owners:** Gérard Capdet and Annick Nagy **Surface area of vineyard:** 700 square metres **Average age of vines:** 30–50 years **Grape production;** 40% Cabernet-Sauvignon, 35% Merlot, 20% Cabernet-Franc, 5% Petit-Verdot **Production:** 2000 bottles **Local sales:** Tel (56) 59 14 92, **and by direct mail:** Château Capdet, 33250 Saint-Julien-Beychevelle

Gérard Capdet's great-grandfather, Gaston Moreau, owned some of Cabernet and Malbec vines above Beychevelle. Besides that, he worked at Château Beychevelle. His son, Fernand, enlarged the plot, allowing Gérard Capdet's father to make a few exchanges. The present surface area is two *'journaux'*, the equivalent of about two days' work, and it is treated in the traditional way. Until 1973 the wines produced by Gérard Capdet and his sister, Annick Nagy, were sold as a generic production. Then they decided to create a label in order to have a 'small quantity of specialized bottled wines'. Looking for a suitably impressive name, they decided finally on 'Clos de la Licorne'. Research, however, revealed that the unicorn had already been used in connection with Burgundy wines. They therefore elected to use their family name to designate their wine, as is the case with the family names of Léoville, Gruaud or Saint-Pierre. This, then, is the origin of Château Capdet, an excellent *cru artisan* from Beychevelle.

One peculiarity of this *cru artisan* is that the grapes are picked by hand on the end of the vine shoots. A wagon with two containers carries the harvest straight to the vats, without any further processing and practically without any pressing or treading. This is a very old method which is now very seldom used, as modern machinery for harvesting collects the grapes, leaving the stems on the branches. After the grapes have been put in the vats, Gérard Capdet allows nature to complete its work. The result is a *'vin de goutte'* which is generally better than average. The wine produced by pressing is kept apart until the end of the secondary fermentation. When it comes to blending, exactly as if the wine were a major *grand cru*, Gérard Capdet estimates the most suitable quantity of pressed wine to be added to the *vin de goutte* to create his *grand vin*. Racking and fining with egg whites are then carried out in the traditional way, and each harvest is matured in casks for at least two years. The result is a well-made wine with a delicious bouquet.

The old vines exist as a means of interpreting the ancient skills, and the great care taken by Gérard Capdet adds a personal touch worthy of a wine expert from the last century. The wine of Château Capdet merits being kept for a lengthy period to achieve full maturity.

Castaing (Domaine)

cru artisan

Commune: Saint-Julien-Beychevelle **Owner:** Mme Cazeau and Jean **Director:** Jean Cazeau **Surface area of vineyard:** 1 hectare approximately **Average age of vines:** 45 years **Grape production:** 60% Cabernet, 30% Merlot, 10% Petit-Verdot **Production:** 3000 bottles **Local sales:** Tel (56) 59 03 13, **and by direct mail:** Domaine Castaing, 33250 Saint-Julien-Beychevelle

At the turn of the century Jean Cazeau's grandfather was head coachman 'at Barton'. (For the last 150 years the locals have not said 'at Léoville-Barton', nor 'at Langoa', but simply 'at Barton'.) During the harvest he exchanged his livery for an apron and was put in charge of the vat-house. Orphaned at an early age, he was more or less brought up by the Bartons, who taught him Irish songs. The edifying words of these songs were difficult to translate into correct French, and sung with a Médoc accent they had a hilarious effect on the audience.

In 1922, when Château Branaire was changing hands, various parcels of land were granted to a small group of wine-producers. Jean Cazeau's father, Léopold Mathias, who was born at Barton, scraped together all his funds and bought 13 rows of vines which are still producing fruit today. In 1929 he planted a further 22 rows on a piece of land which he bought from the Barton estate. In 1956 about a third of this small estate was destroyed by frost. Replanting was essential. In 1965, Jean Cazeau was able to buy 250 square metres, subsequently enlarged by a further 50 square metres. In 1980 a neighbour agreed to sell 180 square metres in three parts, and two of these were exchanged in order to allow the property to be united. As a result of this patchwork, the Domaine de Castaing now has a total area of precisely 1 hectare 80 square metres and 35 centiares. His neighbours are Ducru-Beaucaillou, Saint-Pierre, Gruaud-Larose, Branaire and Léoville Las Cases.

Jean Cazeau is the local hairdresser. His wife produces wine at Château Branaire and their daughter Florence, who is in her early twenties, runs the family grocery shop. This is the second on the right in Beychevelle after the curve at the end of the town, just before you reach Gruaud-Larose. As he does all the work himself, Jean Cazeau has very low overheads. He does not, being a modest man, count the cost of his own time. As the average age of the vines is quite high, yield is small (4 *tonneaux* in good years). From this he produces between 3000 and 4000 bottles. During the harvest, his wife recruits a few friends and acquaintances from Branaire. Twenty pickers start on a Sunday morning and 'by 3 o'clock everything is in order'. The grapes are put into a hand press which does not extract all the juice but succeeds in obtaining the best. (The travelling distiller who produces marc must make a fortune with the grape stems and skins from this source, as they are so rich.) The wine is then taken from the vats after three weeks of maceration and put into casks in M. Cazeau's small *chai*. The total quantity is extremely small but the perfume is good. This is a very good sign as old, unclean casks create an unfavourable impression as soon as you enter a *chai*.

The Domaine de Castaing belonging to Jean Cazeau produces a good, clean wine with a fine bouquet and tannin content. It is a more pronounced type of the 'Saint-Julien Cabernet'. It should be ordered as soon as it is bottled (in general two years after the harvest) and should be allowed to rest in your cellar for as long as possible. The wine is worth waiting for: I promise you that it will keep all its promises.

Ducru-Beaucaillou (Château)

Commune: Saint-Julien-Beychevelle **Owner:** Jean-Eugène Borie **Directors:** Jean-Eugène and Xavier Borie **Chief grower:** André Faure **Maître de chai:** René Lusseau **Surface area of vineyard:** 50 hectares (total property 150 hectares) **Average age of vines:** 30 years **Grape production:** 65% Cabernet-Sauvignon, 25% Merlot, 5% Cabernet-Franc, 5% Petit-Verdot **Production:** 150,000–200,000 bottles **Retail sales:** All the major firms in Bordeaux, Libourne, etc.

2ᶜ cru classé

Jean-Eugène Borie and his family are the lords of Ducru-Beaucaillou. Together with Ronald Barton at Langoa and Henri Martin at Gloria, I believe that they are the only owners of a *grand cru* in Saint-Julien who live permanently in their property, treating it as a stately home. Some will see this as a nostalgic anachronism, while others will admire them in view of the numerous obligations which such a choice nowadays entails. In 1941 Jean-Eugène's father, Francis Borie, bought Ducru-Beaucaillou from the Desbarats de Burke family who had owned it for twelve years. The following year he decided to go and inspect the harvests at his new residence. The children were delighted and the family installed itself in this château as well as it could despite a distinct lack of comfort and a complete absence of electricity. They expected to stay for not more than six weeks, but they are still there. They became very involved with the improvements and decided to stay on permanently, giving the place life and carrying out the alterations and modernization which give it its charm today.

Until the eighteenth century the site was called Maucaillou, a name frequently found in Médoc. It was part of the barony of Beychevelle and depended on the lordship of La Marque. As with many *crus classés,* it was only in about 1760 that the reputation of the wine became established. At that time it belonged to a certain Bergeron, who signed his label with his own name (a tradition which still exists with the brand of Château Lamothe-Bergeron at Cussac). It is not known if the name of Beaucaillou appeared in the time of Bergeron or in that of his successor, Bertrand Ducru, who in 1795 definitively established the Ducru-Beaucaillou appellation, an association of names which would excite philology experts. At that time the buildings on the estate were more modest than today, as they did not include a residence for the owner. Moreover the *cru* did not claim the title of 'château' and for many years the label bore only the description 'Ducru-Beaucaillou'.

By his marriage to Marie Dulasson, Bertrand Ducru had two children. One was

In 1878 Nathaniel Johnston added two Victorian towers to the château.

J.-B. Gustave, who married the young and wealthy widow of Jean-Baptiste Du Luc, whose name we can find on the label of Château Branaire. The other was Marie-Louise, wife of Antoine Ravez, whose father Auguste was the famous lawyer after whom a street is named in Bordeaux. He was *député* for the Gironde from 1816 to 1829 and became an Under Secretary of State and president of the Chambre des Députés. Having been a passionate defender of the freedom of the press, he subsequently became its fierce adversary. Charles X ennobled him and Louis XVIII once said of him: 'Nature created him and then destroyed the mould'. Although his name was never directly attached to that of Ducru-Beaucaillou, it would seem that the influence and contacts of Auguste Ravez played an important part in the development of the *cru*, especially during the period of the 1855 classification.

Finally, to clarify the situation, Marie-Louise Ducru-Ravez bought the entire estate at auction in May 1860. She sold it again in March 1866 to the wife of Nathaniel Johnston, who was born a Dassier, and who bought the property with her own funds. This, however, did not prevent Nathaniel Johnston from feeling very much at home at Ducru-Beaucaillou, and he introduced many technical improvements. This civil engineer from the Ecole polytechnique and the Ecole des Mines was a man full of curiosity, passionately involved with progress and new techniques. He took it into his head to introduce a champagne process to the great wines of Médoc. He transported his harvest across the river and, using the old quarries of Bourg-sur-Gironde, produced a range of sparkling wines. Some of them were called 'Sparkling Ducru'.

In about 1878, just before the onset of phylloxera, mildew appeared in the south-west of France. No one was able to combat this disease and the producers with great consternation saw their finest vineyards wither. (Ten years later, when the phylloxera reached its climax, the situation was even worse.) It so happened that the manager of Ducru-Beaucaillou, a man called David, had many problems with thieves stealing grapes, and other intruders who entered the vineyard. He created a concoction based on copper sulphate with which he painted, in a blue-green colour, the young shoots of the vines most vulnerable to unexpected visitors. To his great astonishment, the mildew 127

The dining room in the Ducru-Beaucaillou residence is a temple dedicated to fine wines and food.

was inhibited on the parts of the vines which he painted. Two professors, Millardet and Gayon (the latter being a student of Pasteur), heard of this phenomenon and took a great interest in this form of 'treatment'. With the help of Skavinski, who was at that time a famous agronomist in Médoc, they persuaded Nathaniel Johnston to apply his mixture on a much wider basis. Johnston agreed, on condition that the experiment was

not carried out on the Ducru-Beaucaillou estate. The treatment was tried out on a much greater scale at another property, Château Dauzac in Labarde (now included in the Margaux appellation). It was a great success, and thus the 'Bordeaux treatment' was born.

In 1820 Bertrand Ducru arranged to have a charming pavilion built in the directoire

M. Jean-Eugène Borie in his wine cellar.

style to make up the principal part of the residence. However, in 1878 Johnston added two square towers which rise on each side of the building like Victorian pavilions. It was said that he was only concerned with the living area which he had created, though the 'ensemble created much more of an effect'. It was also said that the label gained ,much in standing from this alteration. As I have previously mentioned the appellation 'Château' Ducru-Beaucaillou is very recent. Alexis Lichine proposed it in the early sixties to Jean-Eugène Borie. Lichine was promoting the advantages of the Bordeaux 'châteaux' in the USA and he was convinced that importers, distributors, retailers and American customers would want more than a brand name, which anybody could invent. Jean-Eugène Borie agreed with this argument, but he did not change his label to a great extent. It does not even include the traditional mention of '*Grand cru classé en 1855*'. This modesty illustrates the conservative spirit that controls events at present in the Ducru-Beaucaillou establishment. The vineyard is maintained according to the strictest rules of traditional Médoc production. It is still planted with 10,000 shoots per hectare and chemical pesticides are forbidden. Vinification is carried out in the classic tradition and a major work of art is often produced.

Among all the *grands crus* of the Saint-Julien appellation, Ducru-Beaucaillou in my opinion is the most consistent in quality from one vintage to another. Perhaps the presence of Professor Emile Peynaud since 1953 is partly responsible for this success. Some credit should also be given to the well-drained pebbly soil. The main *chai* is situated beneath the château. This arrangement allows the owner to sleep in peace . . . even if Ducru-Beaucaillou is a difficult name for foreigners to pronounce. A very simple label with the name of 'La Croix' is used for wine from young plants or from the less successful vats. This shows the very strict and selective policy of the Borie family. 'Seen from the river, between the jetties of Beychevelle and Saint-Julien, the Château Ducru-Beaucaillou produces a grandiose effect.' When you drink this wine at table, between the roast and the cheese, it has the same effect.

Finegrave (Château)

cru artisan

Commune: Saint-Julien-Beychevelle **Owner:** André Leclerc **Surface area of vineyard:** 500 square metres in the property, 350 square metres on lease **Average age of vines:** 20 years **Grape production:** 60% Cabernet-Sauvignon, 30% Merlot, 10% Cabernet-Franc and Petit-Verdot **Production:** 4000–5000 bottles **Local sales:** Tel (56) 59 15 63, **and by direct mail:** André Leclerc, 33250 Saint-Julien-Beychevelle

André Leclerc is a tough character. His Lorraine origins can be traced in the angle of his jaw, the steely look in his eyes and the strength of his character. His father worked in Désiré Cordier's cellars at Toul, and was then asked by the latter to go to Saint-Julien. In 1922 the whole family moved to Médoc. One daughter was born at Toul and André was born at Château Talbot. He was brought up in the wine trade, about which he is very knowledgeable. From 1937 to 1939 he took a course at the Ecole pratique d'Agriculture at Blanquefort. Subsequently he worked for Henri Lemaire (formerly director of the Maison Cordier) at the Châteaux du Pevrat et Suau in Capian. This period of exile on the other bank of the Garonne in the Côtes de Bordeaux lasted for nine years. His uncle Merlet, formerly owner of the Moulin de la Bridane in Saint-Julien, gave him some rows of vines as a present. A few purchases of parcels of land enlarged this little kingdom to the extent of half a hectare. Furthermore, Mme Nomard leased to him 350 square metres. The wine of Château Finegrave is produced 'at Barton', where André Leclerc has been *maître de chai* since 1959. His wine is stocked separately, with the blessing of Major Ronald who is not averse to tasting it from time to time. However, André Leclerc will shortly be taking his well-earned retirement. He is not sure as yet if he will keep his vineyard. In my opinion he should be encouraged to do so, because if this man, who for twenty-five years has had the importance of high priest of Léoville-Barton and Langoa, does not know how to make good wine, I am tempted to ask if there is anyone else in Saint-Julien who understands the business. His prices are also very reasonable; you should make the most of the opportunity. The wine of André Leclerc is like its master – pure and hard.

Glana (Château du)

Commune: Saint-Julien-Beychevelle **Owner:** G. F. A. Meffre **Manager and maître de chai:** Jean Ardiley **Chef de culture:** Jean Andron **Surface area of vineyard:** 42 hectares (total property 42 hectares) **Average age of vines:** 18 years **Grape production:** 70% Cabernet-Sauvignon and Cabernet-Franc, 25% Merlot, 5% Petit-Verdot **Production:** approximately 240,000 bottles **Local sales:** Some bottles to passing customers, Tel (56) 59 06 47 **Retail sales:** exclusively from SDVF, 20 rue Ferrière, 33000 Bordeaux

cru bourgeois supérieur

In a region of wine-preciosity Château Glana introduces a rational contrast. The first sight of the estate buildings makes you realize that they are different from traditional *chais*. Ampelopsis leaves almost cover the grey plaster walls, creating an anachronistic touch on the left-hand side of the main road between Beychevelle and Château Langoa, opposite the local football ground. Large red letters in relief on the front wall give the name Château du Glana. If a visit to some of the *grands crus* can be intimidating to the casual visitor because of the grandeur of the complex, the visitor to Glana may hesitate because of the austerity of the site. There are no gardens, no clusters of flowers,

The buildings of Château du Glana extend like breakwaters in the ocean.

no trees, no stone gateway to greet you. There is no sign of any welcome for the tourist. A white placard indicates the 'office' which gives on to a courtyard which is as bleak as a barracks cloakroom. The lack of charm outside is continued inside where there is no decoration at all. Don't bother to look for local antiques or for any sort of reception office, however rustic; or for lighting made of cask bases, or for old vine roots, or old engravings, which normally form part of the décor of Médoc *chais*. Monastic austerity shrouds the estate office which is at the end of a vast, long, concrete corridor lined with pallets and cases. At right angles there is a vat-house, which is used both for making wine and for holding stock. Some of the vats are made of cement, others of stainless steel. Everything is clinically clean and only the smell of the place lets you know the use of the equipment. Here the business is making wine, not creating folklore.

This Saint-Julien *cru bourgeois* has belonged for twenty years to the Meffre family, run by M. Gabriel Meffre. This gentleman, who resides throughout the year in the Vaucluse, treats the Glana vineyard as a commercial enterprise for producing a good profit, with no need for expensive and useless embellishments. Gabriel Meffre has important garden centres in the south of France and is a modern agronomist. He discovered Médoc by visiting the area to sell his products. His first purchase was the Château La Commanderie at Saint-Estèphe, then Glana and Lalande at Saint-Julien and Plantey at Pauillac. He comes to inspect his estates two or three times a year, sometimes accompanied by his sons Jean-Paul and Claude who show some interest in wine-producing. Contact with the territory, its people and the environment stops there. Glana is intended for profit, not for pleasure.

The vines, which are strong and healthy, are grown on all available space, and the

cultivation is intensively mechanized. The vines are treated with everything necessary and are harvested with the most up to date machinery. Various parcels of land grouped around a central hub form the terraces. This land was long ago detached from Château Saint-Pierre under the name of Château du Glana. The château is in fact a country house, attractive in a rather severe way. It was built in 1870 by Nadeau, an architect from the town of La Blaye, who was commissioned by a M. Cayx. It was originally called the Chalet Saint-Pierre and its vineyard was not more than 3 hectares. After changing hands several times it became the possession of M. and Mme Kaelin, who kept the use of it after the sale to M. Gabriel Meffre. Today the Glana estate is fifteen times larger than its original size. This, however, does not detract from the quality of the wine produced under its label. In fact, the opposite is true.

Although, as we have seen, the methods of growing and production have broken with regional tradition, we must recognize the high quality of recent vintages. In 1932, the Château du Glana was admitted to the ranks of *crus bourgeois supérieurs* for Médoc. The fifty years which followed did nothing to improve the *cru*, and its reputation had weakened at the time when Gabriel Meffre took it over. We must judge from the evidence. If, even ten years ago, Glana could not claim to compete with the *grands crus* of the locality, then substantial progress has now been made. In 1978, the Syndicat des Crus Grands bourgeois et Crus bourgeois du Médoc included the Château du Glana in its order of 'Palmarès syndical'. Since then, it has become one of the eighteen *Crus bourgeois exceptionnels du Médoc*. Personally, I find that the last three years of Glana have been particularly successful, although I would criticize the predominance of the Cabernet grape which is always a little aggressive, and the fact that the wine has not been aged in the cask. The Château du Glana label is sometimes replaced by a second brand called the Marquis de Lalande.

Gloria (Château)

cru bourgeois

Commune: Saint-Julien-Beychevelle **Owner:** Henri Martin **Director:** Henri Martin **Manager:** Jean-Louis Triaud **Chef de culture:** Maurice Andron **Maître de chai:** Jean-Marie Galey-Berdier **Surface area of vineyard:** 50 hectares (total property 55 hectares) **Average age of vines:** 25 years **Grape production:** 65% Cabernet-Sauvignon, 25% Merlot, 5% Cabernet-Franc, 5% Petit-Verdot **Production:** 300,000 bottles **Local sales:** Tel (56) 59 08 18, **and by direct mail:** Château Gloria, 33250 Saint-Julien-Beychevelle **Retail sales:** Several merchants in Bordeaux

The façade of Château Gloria.

The Château Gloria vineyard was 'invented' (in the Latin sense of the word) by Henri Martin in 1942. The creation of this new *cru* is the result of solid wine-producing experience, of being constantly present at the estate and of deep scientific knowledge. The name Gloria belongs to a piece of land at Beychevelle where the Martin family house was built.

Henri Martin, whom we have already discussed at length, has not attempted, in this presentation of a Saint-Julien appellation, to create a false history for his *cru*. On the contrary, he is proud of the fact that Gloria is a distinct, separate creation. When he thought up the imaginary personage of Paulin Desquet, this was more of a joke than a display of local folklore. Since the last war many people have tried, either physically or metaphorically, to reach the goal which Henri Martin had fixed for himself. Very few have succeeded; and in any case none better than he, in this second half of the twentieth century, has achieved in such a 'glorious' manner the creation of a wine estate which is considered to have great prestige and is universally recognized.

For the last three centuries the Martin family have been labourers or *hommes de chai* in Saint-Julien and Beychevelle. Henri Martin was born at Gruaud-Larose, where his grandfather was *maître de chai*. His father decided to become a cooper and established himself in 1918 on his savings of 30,000 francs. In 1922, Colonel Kappelhoff, owner of the Château Saint-Pierre, asked him to become his *maître de chai*, and later the manager of the estate. Henri worked with his father and they bought together, at their own cost, some *chais* near the old cask-making factory. They also bought some small areas of vines. At the time of the Popular Front in 1936, Martin Senior, who had a violent character which would not allow any discussion, was outraged by the demands of the union workers who stipulated a general strike for all Médoc employees. His own employees were better paid than their colleagues from other estates and were relatively satisfied with their lot. Nevertheless they joined in the strike from a sense of working-class solidarity. In a fury, Alfred Martin sold all his land and kept only the family buildings. This event was for him the most severe blow of his life, as it affected

At Château Gloria the wine matures well even without these superb oak vats.

his most personal democratic and republican convictions. After what he called the 'tragi-comedy' of the Popular Front, he became very depressed, and the man who had been a rather jovial radical socialist changed into a moralizing extremist. The Martin family, however, remained united. To earn a living Alfred and Henri Martin took over a local food cooperative.

In 1942, M. Cazes Senior from Pauillac, who did a little financing, offered the Martin family the possibility of purchasing 6000 *pieds* of vines in Saint-Julien, near the family house. At that time vines were planted per square metre. There were 10,000 plants to the hectare, and 6000 *pieds* corresponded to 6000 square metres of land. The offer was made to Henri Martin. Although almost 40 years of age he still absolutely respected his father's authority. He therefore asked Cazes to wait while he discussed the offer with his father. Alfred was busy playing cards with his friends in a secret retreat which he had set up above the old cask factory. The manager of Ducru-Beaucaillou, the last boatman from Beychevelle, and a visitor from Pagnol were present. Just as Martin was at a critical stage in the game, his son appeared at the top of the ladder to discuss the proposal. His father told him to clear out and the son sheepishly returned to see the financier. After an hour of hesitation, he accepted the offer, especially as part of the purchase could be paid on credit. That night at dinner no one dared to utter a word at the Martin table. When the meal was over, his father cast a cold glance at Henri and asked him how events had turned out. Henri Martin, without beating about the bush, told him what had happened. His father exploded and telling the family to act as witnesses, he shouted: 'And how do you think you are going to pay for your vines?' Everyone went to bed and early the next morning father woke his son saying: 'Right, my friend, let's go and see these vines.' And it was thus that Gloria saw the light. Thanks be to heaven.

Bit by bit, Henri bought all the vines he could possibly afford. One day during the war, he drove Armand Achille-Fould to Arcachon in the small truck which he had bought for the food co-operative. During the trip, he asked the owner of Beychevelle to sell him an isolated piece of land. The deal was finalized and served as an example for dozens of similar purchases from all the owners of *crus* in Saint-Julien. From this jumble Henri Martin succeeded in creating one single property, and his enthusiasm for advertising did the rest. He succeeded in creating a *cru* with a good reputation, one which was known to every wine enthusiast as being extremely reliable. The *New York Times Magazine* of 14 November 1976 reported that

> ... when the chapter of the Commanderie du Bontemps-de-Médoc in New York held its annual banquet in a restaurant in the city, a wine was served which had a fine ruby colour and a distinguished bouquet. This attracted the attention as soon as the wine was served. It could also be described as having finesse, that is to say it was both bold and subtle, aggressive and delicate. It was full and rounded without any sharpness and produced an explosion of taste in the mouth, and with a smooth finish. This was Château Gloria 1961 and the guests doubtless helped in advertising its reputation. The choice of wine, however, was no accident. Henri Martin had contacted the organizers and presented them with 15 cases.

Nowadays Henri Martin, helped by his daughter and her husband Jean-Louis Triaud, controls five different wine labels from Saint-Julien, plus some 'minor' products from the Haut-Médoc, such as Cussac. In this collection can be found, apart from Châteaux Gloria and Saint-Pierre, the Châteaux Bel-Air, Peymartin and Haut-Beychevelle Gloria.

Having been president of the CIVB, of the Girondins of Bordeaux and administrator of Château Latour, Henri Martin has now become less active, conserving his energies for those interests which constitute his life – his family, his wine and the Commanderie du Bontemps and the Grand Conseil du Vin de Bordeaux. One day, perhaps, in place of the monster bottle which decorates the bend of the road at Beychevelle, a statue will be erected to the 'mayor–wine-producer' of Saint-Julien. It is one thing to buy a *cru*: it is quite another to generate one.

Gruaud Larose (Château)

Commune: Saint-Julien-Beychevelle **Owner:** Société civile du Château Gruaud-Larose **Director:** Jean Cordier **Manager:** Georges Pauli **Chef de culture:** Henri Puzos **Maître de chai:** Lucien Moreau **Surface area of vineyard:** 82 hectares (total property 130 hectares) **Average age of vines:** 35 years **Grape production:** 64% Cabernet-Sauvignon, 24% Merlot, 9% Cabernet-Franc, 3% Petit-Verdot **Production:** 400,000 bottles **Direct mail:** Château Gruaud-Larose, 33250 Saint-Julien-Beychevelle, Tel (56) 59 27 00 **Retail sales:** Ets Cordier, quai de Paludate, 33000 Bordeaux

2e *cru classé*

The gardens of Château Gruaud-Larose are always ready for the photographer.

In the early part of the eighteenth century the de Gruaud family made an inventory of some areas of stony ground at Beychevelle. It was at a time when the 'planting fury' had seized well-known inhabitants of Bordeaux. The civilian nobility were in particular attacked by this mania to produce wine. The Gruaud brothers, one of them an ecclesiastic and the other a magistrate, were both infected and united their territory to create one of the largest vineyards of the time, which was first called Fond-Bedeau. The harvests were divided in two and the office archives of the merchant house of Lawton mentions sales which took place alternately in the name of Abbé Gruaud and Chevalier de Gruaud. The strong personalities of the owners helped to create the fame of the wine and built up the reputation of the territory in Saint-Julien de Rignac, where the Gasq family at Léoville and the Brassier family at Beychevelle were exercising their talents as Sunday wine-producers. There is a story that the Chevalier de Gruaud had a tower build in the middle of his vines in order to check on the people working for him and to count the number of missing plants, so that he could replace them as soon as possible. A large mast was erected in front of the vat-house, not for the purpose of saluting his neighbour at Beychevelle but for hoisting the flags of those foreign countries that bought his wine. When the harvest produced solid, full-bodied wines, Gruaud hoisted the English flag. When the flow of wine proved to be 'in the Dutch taste' everybody was advised of this by the sight of the national colours of that country flying at the mast.

Gruaud was not good at selling and would lower his price if the buyer hesitated to pay what was first asked. In 1756 the fiscal administration of Bordeaux records that 'Monsieur Gruaud of Saint-Julien in Lamarque, inscribed on the election list of Bordeaux citizens, has produced 60 *tonneaux* of first-class wine in 1752 and 1753. They were sold at a price of between 700 and 800 pounds the *tonneau*. This was a high price at the time and placed Gruaud at the head of the list of 2e *crus*, right behind Lafite, Latour and Margaux. In the 1760s the fame of the *vin de Gruaud* was at its peak. All those who considered themselves fashionable had to have it in their cellars.

On the death of the Chevalier de Gruaud in 1778, his daughter, who was married to Joseph-Sébastien de La Rose, inherited the estate and the name was changed to La

All the buildings are impeccably maintained.

Rose. J.-S. de La Rose was the president of the *Présidial* (tribunal) and lieutenant-general of the *Sénéchaussée* (seneschal's court) of Guyenne. He was a skilled producer of high-quality wines and maintained the *cru* of Gruaud Larose at the top of the aristocracy of great Médoc Châteaux. In 1787 the future third president of the United States of America, Thomas Jefferson, made a study visit to Bordeaux on behalf of President Monroe. Reference is often made to the detailed report which he wrote and which still serves as a reference for the owners of the most distinguished vineyards, as

M. Lucien Moreau, maître de chai *at Gruaud-Larose, carrying out the ritual of decantation.*

it was regarded as an official classification until 1855. Jefferson places La Rose immediately after the 1e crus and equal to Rauzan and Léoville. In 1815, the shipper Lawton wrote that 'the wine of Larose is the most substantial, yet fragrant and mellow, of all the great wines of Saint-Julien.' During the nineteenth century the estate was divided in two and the distinctive names of the new owners were adopted. They were Gruaud-Larose Sarget, from the name of Baron Sarget de Lafontaine, and Gruaud-

The wooden cases still carry their aristocratic design.

Larose Faure, the name of the Faure Bethmann family, who were connected with the Balguerie and the Stuttemberg families (famous merchants for Chartrons wines).

During the 1855 classification, the jury put Gruaud Larose with the two Rauzan and the three Léoville wines, placing them all in the fifth place of the 2e *crus*, while mentioning individually the three owners: Bethmann, Sarget and Boisgerard. For more than fifty years wine enthusiasts endlessly discussed the respective merits of the different labels. General opinion was more in favour of Gruaud-Larose Faure, but this type of discussion, so popular with wine specialists, only served to maintain the reputation of the principal brand.

In 1914 my grandfather, Fernand Ginestet, was a warden on the border of the property belonging to Désiré Cordier, in the region of Toul in Lorraine. Désiré Cordier then owned a prosperous business in bulk wines. He had obtained the 'contract of the century' by succeeding in supplying the French Government. Just think of it: our brave soldiers could not guard the Vosges without their quarter litre of red wine twice a day. Désiré Cordier invited Fernand Ginestet to take a glass with him. They were chatting away and the gentleman from Bordeaux described in detail to the gentleman from Lorraine the business of producing wine in the Gironde. The latter decided to protect his family from the dangers of Germanic invasion and took them to Bordeaux. In 1917 Cordier bought Gruaud-Larose Sarget from Adrienne Laville, Baronness Sarget de Lafontaine. One year later, just at the end of the war, he also bought Château Talbot for his son Georges, and thus the Cordier family really became part of Bordeaux. Désiré Cordier and Fernand Ginestet were friends for a very long time.

It took almost twenty years for Cordier to reunite Gruaud Larose. The occasion arose in 1934 when the Faure heirs wished to settle their affairs. Désiré Cordier was not one to miss such an opportunity and he bought all the parts of the estate. After more than a century the property regained its original unity, exactly within the boundaries formed by the Chevalier de Gruaud. Since then the label has hardly changed and its impressive motto has reached every part of the world: 'The king of wines, the wine of kings'.

The situation of the Gruaud Larose vineyard is superb. Some of the slopes face south-east, opposite the 'Jalle du Nord'. They terminate in a plateau of deep, dense, stony soil, between Branaire and Lagrange. The château, which is in directoire style, is situated in the centre of a garden in the French style which is always maintained to perfection, as if it were a cover illustration for *House and Garden* (dogs and tourists do not even dare to walk on the lawns). The *chais* and other buildings are worthy of the private museum of a Texas millionaire. There is a collection of old bottles in the cellars illustrating almost two centuries of the history of the best vintages from the *cru*.

The wine of Gruaud Larose is one of the most substantial in the Saint-Julien appellation. Its natural richness has, of course, made the fortune of its owner. (It was not by chance that a French financial group recently took an 'interest' in this production.) Virile with the strength of its tannin and feminine in the subtle charms of its bouquet, Gruaud Larose represents both aspects of classical beauty.

Haut-Beychevelle Gloria (Château) ⚇
→ Gloria

Jaugaret (Domaine du)

cru artisan supérieur

Commune: Saint-Julien-Beychevelle **Owner:** Héritiers Fillastre (Jean-François, Claudine, Gérard and Pierre, **Chief partner** Jean-François Fillastre **Surface area of vineyard:** 1.3 hectares **Average age of vines:** Approximately 50 years **Grape production:** 70% Cabernet, 25% Merlot, 5% Malbec **Production:** Approximately 3000 bottles **Local sales:** Tel (56) 59 09 71, **and by direct mail:** Domaine du Jaugaret, 33250 Saint-Julien-Beychevelle

Jean Fillastre, who died in January 1983 at the age of 90, had four heirs to share among themselves the rights to about four *journaux* of land in the AOC area of Saint-Julien. However, Claudine, Gérard and Pierre have left the locality and are not involved with agricultural work. Jean-François has remained at Beychevelle, where he lives with his mother. This 40 year old bachelor intends to maintain the well-established roots of his family. There is a document in existence proving that the family was already living in Sanct-Julius de Rinhac in 1654. It is not often that you find a family which has been permanently in one area for more than three centuries and Jean-François Fillastre has more or less openly declared that he wishes to keep this spiritual heritage going. On the material level, the heritage is quite modest. It includes a house on the outskirts of the town of Beychevelle, a vegetable garden with a chicken run and a *chai* with attached vat-house.

Jean-François Fillastre's father was a powerful man, tall, lean and gnarled like a branch of an old Cabernet vine. He had his own strong ideas on the art of making good wine. When animals were no longer used in agriculture, he agreed to cultivate his vineyard with a cultivator, but this was his only concession to mechanization. Imagine girdling by hand four times a year about 1.30 hectares of vines scattered through eight parcels of land! Nowadays Jean-François makes use of a small tractor but, as in his father's time, all the other work is carried out by hand. At the time of the harvest the brothers and their sister return to the estate, together with their families. It is an

A portrait of Jean Fillastre painted in 1924 by his brother, Fillastre-Dumont.

occasion for getting together. An antique press crushes the grapes and the must is put into the wooden fermentation vat which can hold 52 hectolitres. (It is very unusual for this to be insufficient but the vat-house contains a second smaller one in case of emergencies . . .) The *chai* is a perfect example of orderliness and tradition. It can house up to three harvests at the same time, since Jean-François Fillastre allows his wine to mature in casks for eighteen months to three years. Bottling is done directly from the tap on the vat and corking is carried out by hand.

The Domaine du Jaugaret certainly possesses the oldest vines of Saint-Julien. Some of the roots are more than a hundred years old. The vineyard has vines of about fifty years of age and the average yield during recent years is less than 30 hectolitres per hectare. Like his father, Jean, Jean-François Fillastre is not afraid of hard work – quite the contrary, in fact, as he complains at present that he does not have enough to keep him busy. When he was 15 years old Jean-François started work at the Domec glass factory in Bordeaux. He chose this trade because the apprentices were given board and 143

In a corner of his chai *Jean-François Fillastre carries out some experiments in fining.*

lodging. He became a glass-blower and practised this tough and demanding trade for twenty-two years, until 1981, when the glass factory closed its doors. Jean Fillastre before him had been chief car mechanic at Packard. His brother, a very gifted painter, had exhibited successfully at the Salon d'Automne and was just beginning to gain a reputation when he was killed in a car accident at the Archevêque bridge in the 1930s. Jean-François Fillastre still has several canvases painted by his uncle which show that he was much more than a gifted amateur.

This young wine-producer of Saint-Julien conceals behind a rough exterior a real local sensibility with noble ideals. For him the preservation of tradition is a permanent goal. He is of an independent nature, and proud of his autonomy: he does not ask for help from anybody. He continues the singleminded attitude of his father and, if the term 'wine made in the old style' still has any meaning, then the label of the Domaine du Jaugaret is a classic example of this tradition. If you ask him how he describes his wine, Jean-François Fillastre will reply, quite simply: 'It is good and made according to the oldest traditions.' That is perfectly true.

La Bridane (Château)

cru artisan supérieur

Commune: Saint-Julien-Bèychevelle **Owner:** Pierre Saintout **Regisseur:** Bruno Saintout **Surface area of vineyard** 17 hectares (total property 17 hectares) **Average age of vines:** 20 years **Grape production:** 55% Cabernet, 45% Merlot **Production:** 80,000 bottles **Local sales:** Tel (56) 59 41 28, **and by direct mail:** Domaine de Cartujac, 33112 Saint-Laurent-Médoc **Retail sales**

It was with a certain pride that Pierre Saintout recalled the ancestry of the families who were estate owners and wine-producers at Saint-Julien. His own family can trace its origins in this parish back to the sixteenth century through the names of Mérie and Gondat Blancau, which are typical of the Médoc. The vineyard is in two parts, one to the west of the village of Saint-Julien and the other at the top of a fine stony slope to the north of the appellation, near the *crus* of Léoville, Pichon Longueville and Latour, by the Juillac stream. The Bridane is the name of the local parish road leading from Saint-Julien to the main road between Saint-Laurent and Pauillac. In former times it was a mule path leading to the Madrac woods, famed for the mushrooms which grew there. It was used for transporting the bark from the oak and pine trees to the port of Saint-Julien and on the return journey the muleteers carried back goods imported through the estuary. These routes, which were formerly vital for the local economy, are now relatively idle, as there is no local custom. The roads running from north to south have replaced the river traffic.

Pierre Saintout, who died only recently, was one of the very last small wine-producers at Saint-Julien. He cultivated his 15 hectares of Cabernet-Sauvignon, Merlot and Petit-Verdot grapes with the care of a gardener choosing his roses for an international exhibition. The same attention was given to his wine-production and to his bottling, which are fine examples of the Médoc tradition in the best sense of the term – that is, with absolute regard for tried and trusted values.

The deep, stony soil of Château La Bridane allows for a great degree of 'filtering'. Because of this there are practically no bad years and vintages have a surprising consistency of quality. When the summers are very warm and dry, the quantity of wine is reduced by a half, but Pierre Saintout's grapes have an exceptional natural concentration. On this type of soil, the vine ages particularly well, plunging its roots deep into the soil to extract from it a sort of essence.

When asked his opinion on recent vintages, Pierre Saintout would hesitate a little before replying in order to whet your appetite. When he decided to speak, however, there was no stopping him. His opinion was as follows:

A wine-producer always replies with pleasure and humility to questions regarding his product. The vintage of 1970 was a very balanced and rounded wine. It will

M. Pierre Saintout: a true inhabitant of Médoc.

mature in about 1982 and will have a long and successful career, and will still be discussed in twenty years' time. The same applies to the 1975 vintage, with an additional qualification, as the wine contains more tannin and will have keeping qualities which will enable it to last for more than thirty years. The 1971 vintage is a lighter wine, but it is well balanced with a distinguished bouquet and remains for a long time on the palate. It is in first-class condition and will remain so for another four or five years. The 1974 vintage should be kept for a little while longer; it has a very delicate bouquet which lingers on the palate, and will still be drunk with pleasure for the next ten years. The 1976 harvest is very similar to that of 1975. It is well balanced, well made but slightly less full-bodied. It will be ready for drinking sooner than the other vintages. The 1978 vintage is a well-rounded wine which will keep well and should be ready for drinking in about three years' time. The 1979 vintage is virile and with a fine colour. It can be compared with the 1978 vintage and will last very well through the seventies. The 1980 vintage is well balanced in tannin and alcohol and will improve on the mediocre reputation which it earned initially. It will be very quick in maturing and will last throughout the decade. The 1981 vintage is one of the great vintages. The wine is well rounded and could rapidly mature in about three years. The 1982 vintage is a gift of nature, and quantity and quality are blended in it. The wine producers compare its potential with that of the vintages 1943–1945–1947. It will be very pleasant when it is young and will have a long life which will be discussed for many years. With regard to the 1983 vintage it is still a little early to discuss it, but it is probably one of the best years of the last half century.

Pierre Saintout was well known in the region. He lived at Saint-Laurent and travelled around the region so much that he seemed to be everywhere at the same time. He was an old style inhabitant of Médoc, the sort who knows what the weather will be like the day after tomorrow. Of course you can enjoy visiting Léoville, Ducru, Gruaud, Branaire and Beychevelle, but Saintout was worth a visit on his own account. Particularly when he asked you to taste his wine.

Lacoufourque (Cru de)

cru artisan

Commune: Saint-Julien-Beychevelle **Owner:** Jean Deba and associates **Surface area of vineyard:** 1.25 hectares **Average age of vines:** Approximately 40 years **Grape production:** 100% Cabernet-Franc **Production:** Approximately 6 *tonneaux* **Retail sales:** All in bulk

Lacoufourque is a very old, small *cru* from Beychevelle which is particularly noted for being entirely planted with Cabernets-Francs. Since the death of his mother, Jean Deba continues to cultivate the family vineyard but problems in the legacy give this small estate an unfortunate lack of security. Jean Deba has therefore decided to carry harvesting and winemaking to their logical conclusion and to sell his wine in casks. There is no label and the wines come under the generic appellation of Saint-Julien. This is regrettable. It is also regrettable that three years ago the Deba family closed the only restaurant in Beychevelle.

La Croix ⚱

→ *Ducru-Beaucaillou*

Lagrange (Château)

3e cru classé

Commune: Saint-Julien-Beychevelle **Owner:** SARL (the Japanese Suntory Group) **Surface area of vineyard:** 56 hectares (total property 162 hectares) **Grape production:** 50% Cabernet-Sauvignon, 50% Merlot **Production:** 250,000 bottles **Visits:** By appointment, Tel (56) 59 23 63 **Retail sales:** Numerous Bordeaux merchants

The year 1899 was excellent for wine. The weather was warm and sunny, from the flowering of the vines to the harvest (which started on 20 August). That year was a great vintage. In Japan, 1899 was also a vintage year. The country of the Rising Sun saw the beginning of a demand for domestic wines. It was the first vintage for the Acadama brand, a liqueur wine rather like port. The Suntory Company was looking for outlets, and found so many and such effective ones that it is now one of the most important and successful distribution companies in the world for wines and spirits. Its consolidated turnover has overtaken that of the Canadian company, Seagram. Suntory produces its own brand of whisky, beers, sparkling drinks and fruit juices, apart from being the second largest producer of Japanese wines, after Mercian. The vines are planted at the foot of Mount Fuji-Yama which is why the wine is called Yamanashi. This is not all: Suntory also owns a laboratory for pharmaceutical research and is developing a line of products to fight cancer. The group owns a chain of more than two

Even in 1926 the men in armour on the Lagrange label looked rather like samurai.

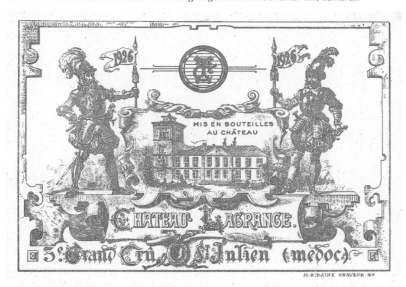

The large park and impressive buildings make Lagrange a fine estate.

hundred restaurants in Japan. In Europe there is a Suntory restaurant in London, in Milan and in Paris on the Champs-Elysées near the Japan Airlines office. In Japan, Suntory is the largest importer of French wines. They sell about 100,000 cases each year.

In 1984 Château Lagrange was purchased by Suntory. The wine was a *3ᵉ cru classé* in 1855, when it belonged to the Cendoya family. Since 1925 it has been in quarantine, so to speak, since its reputation was the lowest of the *grands crus* of Médoc. In spite of many parcels of land having been sold off during the last half century, the Château Lagrange estate still covers a large surface area. Several Saint-Julien *crus* have been extended at its cost, and the property, which covered 300 hectares a hundred years ago, now has only 157. However, this territory, belonging to one owner, is still one of the most important in all of Médoc. The surface area at present planted with vines is about half of its potential. Suntory has established a programme to replant some of the fine, stony terraces and forecasts 100 hectares of vines by 1987.

In the nineteenth century, the opinion of wine specialists on Lagrange differed greatly. Criticism was made of its rapid growth in the hands of the banker Cabarrus who bought it in 1796. Then John Lewis Brown (of Cantenac-Brown in Margaux) took it over, enlarging the estate even further and building most of the *chais*. Finally, Charles-Marie Tanneguy, Count Duchâtel and minister of Louis-Philippe, became the owner in 1842. Historians of the period maintain that the important position of Tanneguy-Duchâtel made it easy for him to have Lagrange promoted to the rank of

the *3^e crus*, although his wines had long been sold as belonging to the *4^e crus*. It has also been said that the owner, assisted by a famous manager called Galos, did everything in his power to improve the quality of the *cru*. In 1852 he installed the first irrigation system which had ever been seen in the Gironde. At the time, of course, trenches were dug by hand and the drains consisted of earthenware pipes buried more than a metre below the surface and joined in sections of 80 centimetres.

It would seem that Chateau Lagrange in the following century was too large to manage. The crisis of the thirties reduced it to a pitiful state. The market for *grands crus* is sensitive and selective. Apart from the quality of a wine sold under a certain label, the quantity offered to traditional customers can saturate the market very rapidly. In a period of economic recession this can lead to collapse. The owner of that period, Manuel Cendoya, tried to diversify his production by creating secondary marks such as Château Saint-Julien, Château La Tour du Roi, Clos des Chartrons, etc. These efforts, far from improving the main brand, dragged it down, and Cendoya survived by selling his property badly, having failed to sell his wine well.

Nowadays it seems likely that Château Lagrange is about to take off on a lap of honour. Suntory has stated that it is prepared to devote all the necessary time, science and finance to achieve this. It had long been a dream of the president of Suntory, Mr Sagi, to purchase a château in Médoc. Ten years ago the company had attempted to buy the Château de Caillavet, in the Côtes de Bordeaux. This Japanese 'invasion' attracted a great deal of attention in the press and the French Government decided to

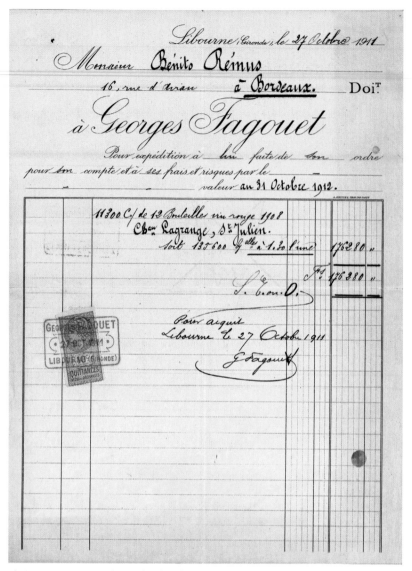

An important invoice: 135,600 bottles of Château Lagrange 1908.

curb the Japanese appetite by forbidding the transaction. Armed with this experience, Mr Sagi handled his second approach with much more discretion and the affair caused little stir. Mr Nagata, who is general manager for the company in France, is extremely discreet about the methods used to obtain government approval. As far as I am concerned (and the affair could have concerned me directly in the past) I find it an excellent idea for a company of this size to take an interest in a part of the Médoc territory. I don't think that anybody loses, including Suntory, I hope. For the present, the declared intention of the new owner is to restore the estate according to tried and tested methods.

Professor Peynaud has already been recruited to take charge of the wine-making. He is a generous man who never says no, and his large heart could well accept an adopted *cru*. It would be particularly interesting to know what amount of the Merlot grape he will use, as this vine at present makes up 50 per cent of the Lagrange vineyard. The proportion is unique in Saint-Julien, which is a bastion of the Carbernet-Sauvignon grape in Médoc. It is quite possible that the quartet of Lagrange-Suntory-Merlots-Peynaud has some surprises in store for us. That, at least, is my own bet. However, we must also reckon with the experience of Michel Delon, who is the administrator for Léoville Las Cases, and the young agricultural engineer, Mr Suzuta. When the vineyard has doubled its surface area, apart from certain territory which has been out of use for fifty years, we shall see what we shall see. The vintage of 1999 for Château Lagrange could well produce a fine bottle to celebrate the centenary of the very honourable Suntory company. Why, you may ask, did the Japanese buy Château Lagrange? The reply: 'to learn about wine'. We should be careful. When a Japanese wishes to learn something, it means that he wishes to give others lessons.

CHATEAU LAGRANGE

S.T JULIEN - MEDOC

La Gravière (Cru de)

cru artisan

CRU DE LA GRAVIÈRE
SAINT-JULIEN
APPELLATION ST-JULIEN CONTROLÉE

Commune: Saint-Julien-Beychevelle **Owner:** Jean-Marie and Henriette Bouin **Surface area of vineyard:** 500 square metres **Average age of vines:** 20 years **Grape production:** 1000 *pieds* Cabernet-Franc; 60% Merlot; Petit-Verdot (small amount) **Production:** At present, only bulk sales to the trade

---

Mme Bouin comes from the Andrivet family and is in dispute with two or three other Beychevelle families regarding her claim to be descended from the most ancient family in the region. We have described earlier in this book how the Andrivet brothers worked as boatmen in the port of Beychevelle towards the end of the last century. Their line is continued through Henriette Bouin, who is proud to let you know that her family has one of the oldest plots in the cemetery. (Saint-Julien cemetery is worth a visit. It is situated in the middle of a vineyard like an extra part of it and has three tombs and two palm trees. It is surrounded by Cabernet vines.) When you speak to this Médoc lady, who comes from the riverside area not the interior of the country, the past is conjured up before your very eyes. She is certainly not of a venerable age, but she wears her ancestors rather like amulets. I would like to pay my respects to this lady by quoting the text of a letter dated 3 November 1882. In this, the firm of G. Coutaut & Eug. Avril of Bordeaux informed M. Robert Jules, an estate owner at Saint-Julien, about the fate of his delivery of sulphide of carbon. The disease of phylloxera was at its height. Every wine-producer was trying to protect himself against the terrible scourge by injecting this chemical into the earth, to a depth of about 40 centimetres at the base of each vine stock. The letter ran as follows:

We acknowledge receipt of your letter of the 2nd of this month. We must inform you, however, that with the best will in the world we are unable to arrange transport to the quay without knowing precisely where the boatman Andrivet will be, so that we can deliver to him the three casks of sulphide of carbon. You should know that it is forbidden to leave this liquid on the quays. If M. Andrivet comes to place the order in the morning and then leaves in the evening we shall probably be able to make the delivery. If at all possible, please notify us the day before. Whenever you place an order in the future, please be so kind as to let us know at which jetty the boatmen will be working. Otherwise it will be impossible for us to arrange transport. Yours truly,
Bosc.
PS. We have just returned from the Fenwick jetty and have seen Andrivet, who will leave tomorrow before midday. When you receive casks in the future, please give us exact dates.

The Andrivet mentioned is probably the great-grandfather or great-great uncle of Henriette Bouin. Her husband is Jean-Marie Bouin, a solid citizen of Nantes with a pre-war moustache. He came to Médoc in 1947 as a foreman with the construction company called La Nantaise. It was he who was responsible for remaking the road from Carcans to Saint-Julien. He became fond of the region and was subsequently in charge of clearing and planting the Jonc estate, near the sea coast. In 1973 he was chosen by Jean Cordier as manager of Château Talbot. His vines extend over half a hectare. He produces little, but excellent wine, which he sells in bulk to the trade, without using his label, although this has been in existence for many years. It would be a good idea if Jean-Marie Bouin could find the time to label his own wine.

Lalande (Château)

cru artisan supérieur

Commune: Saint-Julien-Beychevelle **Owner:** M. Gabriel Meffre, who is administrator of la Société d'Exploitation du Château Lalande **Manager:** Jean Ardiley **Surface area of vineyard:** 30 hectares **Average age of vines:** 15 years **Grape production:** 70% Cabernet-Sauvignon, 30% Merlot **Production:** Approximately 100 *tonneaux* **Retail sales:** Both with and without the château label

---

Château Lalande has 30 hectares of young vines between Chateaux Lagrange and Talbot, at the side of the road between Beychevelle and Saint-Laurent. The stony soil is dense and compact. There is also a quantity of black sand which marks the end of the upper terraces of Saint-Julien. The vineyard, which came into existence because of the sale of a section of Château Lagrange in 1964, was included at the time by M. Gabriel Meffre in the estate of Château du Glana. Without changing its owner it has once again been legally separated so that now it is run by a commercial company and has a private label which has been specifically designed for it. This brand is therefore a recent creation and covers about a third of the Meffre production in the Saint-Julien appellation. Their methods of growing, wine-production and maturing are exactly the same as at Glana, but both estates declare their vintages independently.

Like Glana, Lalande uses a high proportion of Cabernet-Sauvignon grapes which produces a rather 'concentrated' type of wine, sometimes high in tannin content. Maturing in casks would be desirable in order to refine this rather rough, harsh raw material. According to the year, a part of the harvest is sold as a generic wine and taken by the trade in bulk. Gabriel Meffre is nowadays practically the only important supplier of Appellation Saint-Julien wine to the commercial houses of Bordeaux. When the wine is bottled at the château, under the Château Lalande label, it can prove to be an attractive purchase for the wine enthusiast and offers good quality for the price.

Lalande-Borie (Château)

cru artisan supérieur

Commune: Saint-Julien-Beychevelle **Owner:** Jean-Eugène Borie **Chef de culture:** André Faure **Maître de chai:** René Lusseau **Surface area of vineyard:** 18 hectares (total property 30 hectares) **Average age of vines:** 14 years **Grape production:** 65% Cabernet-Sauvignon, 25% Merlot, 10% Cabernet-Franc **Production:** 50,000–95,000 bottles **Retail sales:** Mainly by the following companies: Dubos frères, Duclot, Dourthe, Johnston at Bordeaux and Coste at Langon

Château Lalande-Borie is a recent creation. In 1970 Jean-Eugène Borie, owner of the Ducru-Beaucaillou estate, had an analysis done of a parcel of 30 hectares of land on the Legrange estate. The chief engineer of the Institut national de la Recherche agronomique made the visit in person and his report confirmed the high agrological quality of this stony slope. The Borie family subsequently found a company to develop the land. The quantity of grape production was studied minutely with the care that is typical of the top-class wine producers. An initial section of 18 hectares was planted in the traditional way.

The Lalande-Borie label is not at all a 'second brand' of Ducru-Beaucaillou. It constitutes a château label on its own, as defined according to classic Bordeaux tradition. This means that the estate must be an *Appellation d'origine* and that the production must take place on the site. New regulations are being worked out to prohibit the use of the name château for secondary brands of a *cru*, allowing only the place name. These are subtle legal arguments which change nothing of the quality of the wine in question. I have often said that French legislation for wine tends to protect the producer rather than the consumer. You can be quite sure, at any event, that when you plan to open a bottle of Château Lalande-Borie it will comply fully with all the regulations. This wine from young plants is more than promising. The highly qualified personnel from Ducru-Beaucaillou are involved with the production, under the direction of Jean-Eugène Borie, whose talents for producing wine have been well known for many years.

The vat-house and the *chais* of Lalande-Borie belonged to the old *cru* of Saint-Louis du Bosc, a brand which no longer exists. During the last century, in the time of Léon Sevaistre, it was a development centre for the Château Saint-Pierre Sevaistre, a Saint-Julien *cru classé* which had a fantastic destiny. The buildings were constructed in about 1880 and are very much in the style of the period. They look rather like the early villas of Soulac and Arcachon. They have now been completely modernized and have the best traditional equipment. There is no owner's residence on the site, but a the complex of buildings looks like a small château. I believe that Jean-Eugène Borie had a very soft spot for this *cru* which he really created himself, rather like a naval captain who is responsible for building his own boat. Without claiming to be a royal 153 barge, like Ducru-Beaucaillou, Lalande-Borie has been well conceived for pleasing the palate. Its reasonable price adds to its charm. It is exactly the type of wine I would store in my cellar to serve to friends as a 'good little Saint-Julien'. This is just my way of putting things, as there are no little wines at Saint-Julien. The adjective here is a term of endearment.

Langoa *(Château)*

3*e* cru classé

Commune: Saint-Julien-Beychevelle **Owner:** GFA des Châteaux Langoa and Léoville Barton **Director:** Anthony Barton **Manager:** André Leclerc, assisted by Michel Raoul who will succeed him **Surface area of vineyard:** 20 hectares (total property 45 hectares) **Average age of vines:** 25 years **Grape production:** 70% Cabernet-Sauvignon, 15% Merlot, 8% Cabernet-Franc, 7% Petit-Verdot **Production:** 70,000 bottles **Direct mail:** Château Langoa, 33250 Saint-Julien-Beychevelle, Tel (56) 59 06 05 **Exclusive distrituion:** Anthony Barton BP No 8, 33450 Saint-Loubes, Tel (56) 20 45 75

In 1971 there was a celebration for the 150th anniversary of the purchase of Langoa by Hugh Barton. On that occasion the Barton family, which still owns this château, published a book written by Cyril Ray, the respected English writer on wines. From this book we learn that Thomas Barton was born in Enniskillen in Ireland in 1695. He was the eldest son of a rich landowner and an important breeder of sheep. In the early eighteenth century an English law was passed which created a monopoly on the import of Irish wool into England and imposed heavy taxes on it in order to protect English breeders. This led to an important smuggling business with France which paid higher prices than were paid by the English for Irish wool, the best quality in Europe. Four-fifths of the production were sold to the Continent illegally and Bordeaux became an important centre for this trade. However, the quantities of gold and money which circulated attracted the attention of the Government. Consequently the Irish sheep breeders asked for payment in casks of wine and cognac, brought back by their own ships. At the age of 20, Thomas Barton left his native Ireland and took up residence in the Chartrons district of Bordeaux where there was a prosperous Anglo-Saxon community.

By 1745 the Barton family were the most important shippers of Bordeaux wine. Two years later, Thomas Barton bought a vineyard at Saint-Estèphe, called the Château Le Boscq. He was an energetic businessman who was well known in the European wine-trade under the nickname of French Tom. He taught the trade to his grandson Hugh who followed him in the business. Local tradition maintains that the wife of William Barton, mother of Hugh,

A miniature of Mme W. Barton after a portrait by Gainsborough.

154

The paintings of the Barton family ancestors go back more than 250 years.

Hugh Barton, a foreign resident, had to apply for a 'resident's card'.

was painted by Gainsborough, but nobody knows what happened to this portrait. In 1786, Hugh Barton joined forces with a Bordeaux merchant called Daniel Guestier. During the 'Terror' Hugh Barton, although he had French citizenship, encountered serious problems with the 'terrifying' representative of the people, Alex Ysabeau. The Barton family were held at the Carmelite convent which was used as a prison. When he was freed Hugh returned to Ireland where he became a successful businessman.

Until the Treaty of Amiens in 1802, the Bordeaux business was administered by Daniel Guestier. The business called Maison Barton et Guestier was founded. Finally Hugh returned to France and was successful in the crazy speculation which took place in the first years of the French Empire. Between 1811 and 1814 the price of wine doubled and so did his fortune. It occurred to him that he should produce wine himself. He considered several properties before deciding to buy Lafite. However, in 1821 he was beaten by the bank of Sir Claude Scott (and his son Samuel, who was declared the legal owner of the estate). Subsequently he bought Château Langoa, and shortly afterwards a small part of the large estate of Léoville. (See section under this name.) In 1845 his fortune amounted to £656,000! He died at the age of 88, in 1854, and was certainly one of the most influential *Seigneurs du vin* of his time.

Château Langoa is on the left-hand side of the D2 road midway between the villages of Beychevelle and Saint-Julien. At this point the traveller will notice a slope descending to the tiny valley of the stream called the Long. We can see here how history and geography blend. If this modest brook had been a *jalle* (or canal with marshy banks) opening on to the river, there would have been two appellations here instead of one, as the water would have formed a wine boundary between Beychevelle in the south and Saint-Julien in the north. This stream was formerly crossed by a ford (*gué*, or *guà* in dialect). From that, it is claimed, is derived the name of Langoa (*Long-gua*), which lies half on either side of the valley eroded in the stony soil by the Long. It is also possible, however, that the name Langoa is derived from *L'anglois*, an inheritance from the Hundred Years War, well before the peaceful invasion by the Irishman, Barton.

Whatever the origin of the name, Langoa is a fine property whose vines produce the same quantity of wine as mentioned in the classification of 1855, which is not the

Château Langoa is one of the most charming houses in Médoc.

case for all the *crus classés*. It is a pity that the main road passes so close to the château. As the road is very straight at this point, drivers are tempted to travel at high speed, not pausing to admire the architecture of the house, which I consider to be one of the most elegant in Médoc. It was built in 1758 by the then owner, Bernard Pontet, who left his name in Médoc with the Château Pontet-Canet. The river front is in pure eighteenth-century Bordeaux style. The great originality of the building lies in the fact that the *chai* used for maturing the wine is situated at ground level beneath the residence, so that no wine can be moved without the knowledge of the owner. There Ronald Barton keeps his treasured personal collection of bottles of Langoa and Léoville, as well as of other great *crus* of Médoc. Other large, traditional *chais* were added in the nineteenth century. The Barton family's recent history can be traced up to Ronald, who is nowadays assisted by his nephew Anthony in the management of the two estates.

Langoa-Barton and Léoville-Barton are owned by one and the same company. The products of the two vineyards, however, have always been kept carefully separate by the owners. The harvests gathered on the estates are processed separately. In fact the two *crus* are never put together. They are treated exactly as if they belonged to two different owners who have reached an agreement on sharing the use of the same equipment and storage facilities. Ronald Barton queries the fairness of the 1855 classification which made Léoville-Barton a *2ᵉ cru*, while Langoa was relegated to the third rank. In general the Château Langoa wines have a little less body than those of Léoville, which makes them ready for drinking sooner. They are, however, better constructed than many of the other Saint-Julien *crus*. This is partly due to the age of the vines and partly due to the vinification process which involves a long maceration.

For obvious reasons the Château Langoa label is best known in Great Britain. It is found less frequently in France and in the northern European countries. Having been the monopoly of the Maison Barton and Guestier for more than 150 years, Langoa is now distributed through several merchants in Bordeaux and is even sold, to some extent, directly in the French market. It is a wine always worth buying.

Léoville Barton (Château)

2e cru classé

Commune: Saint-Julien-Beychevelle **Owner:** GFA des Châteaux Langoa and Léoville Barton **Director:** Anthony Barton **Manager:** André Leclerc, assisted by Michel Raoul who will succeed him **Surface area of vineyard:** 40 hectares (total property 130 hectares) **Average age of vines:** 25 years **Grape production:** 70% Cabernet-Sauvignon, 15% Merlot, 8% Cabernet-Franc, 7% Petit-Verdot **Production:** 140,000 bottles **Direct mail:** Château Léoville Barton, 33250 Saint-Julien-Beychevelle, Tel (56) 59 06 05 **Retail sales:** Several merchants in Bordeaux

After buying Langoa, Hugh Barton wished to consolidate his position as an estate-owner in Saint-Julien by purchasing other neighbouring vineyards. Until the French Revolution the estate of Léoville was the largest in Médoc. The property was owned by several of the descendants of Blaise Antoine Alexandre de Gasq, 'lord of Léoville'. Two of them were also connected with the de Beauvoir family and with the Las Cases (see Léoville Las Cases), whose emigration involved the confiscation of their property and the division of the vineyard. Between 1922 and 1926, Hugh Barton, who was then associated with Daniel Guestier, personally bought 35 hectares, that is about a quarter of the Léoville estate, which he distinguished from the other lots by calling it Léoville Barton. He did not bother to give his label a real stone château since he already owned Langoa and the commercial estate buildings. It is thought that his original intention was to transfer this purchase to his grandfather once he had finally succeeded in cashing the indemnity due to foreign émigrés. His grandfather, however, apparently deposited funds with a lawyer in Paris who advised him to invest elsewhere. Hugh Barton then decided to keep the estate and it was passed on to his heirs during the second half of the nineteenth century.

Ronald Barton arrived in Bordeaux in 1924, when he was 22 and had just finished his university studies. In 1927 his father died in a hunting accident and so Ronald

MM. Ronald and Anthony Barton.

became the sole heir to Léoville Barton and Langoa. In association with Daniel Gues-tier, a descendant of the one mentioned previously, he ran the commercial house of Barton and Guestier, while at the same time looking after the commercial development of his vineyards. In 1940 Ronald Barton was advised by the British Embassy to leave France for England. Like his ancestor, Hugh, who more than a century before had entrusted his affairs to Guestier, he did the same and managed to get on board a South American ship carrying frozen meat, taking with him only a case half filled with personal belongings and a few thousand francs in his pocket. For sentimental reasons he joined the Royal Inniskilling Fusiliers, as Enniskillen had been the homeland of his 159

The paved courtyard of Léoville Barton has not changed in a hundred years.

ancestors. He was immediately given the position of liaison officer with the Free
French forces, in particular in the Middle East and North Africa, where he represented
the Allied Forces on the staff of General de Lattre de Tassigny.

He returned to France in August 1944, when he landed at Saint-Raphael. During
his absence his associates had continued to manage his affairs. They had succeeded in
persuading the occupying forces that the Irish and not English origins of Barton
qualified him as neutral. Because of this, his estates were not confiscated. On his return
Major Ronald Barton, covered with distinguished decorations, including the *Légion*

d'honneur, found his vineyards in a pitiful state. As with all the properties of the region, lack of money had prevented sufficient maintenance from being carried out. Certain parcels of land had not been ploughed for three years. The vines had been neglected or insufficiently cared for, and were in a terrible condition. At least a quarter of the vineyard should have been pulled up. However, with the patience and stubborness typical of his race, he decided to bring everything back into good condition, so as to avoid having to plant too many young vines. During three consecutive years he lavished such care on his vines that they recovered and started to produce excellent

161

vintages. This explains why there was no drop in quality at Léoville Barton and Langoa during the fifties, while many of the other Médoc estates had to undertake massive replanting of their vineyards.

Although Léoville Barton and Langoa have many characteristics in common, their wines are not similar. In fact, the types could be much closer since they are immediate neighbours in the area of Saint-Julien. The proportions of grape varieties used are the same and the processes of making the wine are carried out in the same way, as are the operations in the vat-houses and in the *chais*. This is a classic example (and to my knowledge unique in the whole of Médoc) illustrating how the micro-agrological factors play a decisive role in determining the potential qualities of a great *cru*. We must also pay tribute to the skill of the owner, who has always respected the individuality of the two labels and who has made it a point of honour to allow nature to accentuate the differences. I am not convinced that a 'French mentality' would reason in this way.

Ronald Barton, known as the Major, is a highly respected figure in the Bordeaux wine trade. He is modest and discreet but also independent. He is a self-contained man whose philosophy and education belong to the eighteenth century. In 1974 he was offered an extremely attractive price for his properties. He could not believe his ears, and peering through his powerful spectacles, his Irish blue eyes wide with astonishment, he said: 'What on earth would I do with all that money?' Although he has spent sixty years of his life in close contact with the French language, which he speaks to perfection, he still has an extraordinary accent which I suspect him of maintaining as an eccentric part of his personality. Ronald Barton is a distinguished man with a very fine palate. In my opinion he is the best judge alive of fine Médoc wines. However, his modesty and his own personal values have never allowed him to become flamboyant. He is very careful to avoid giving any definitive statement, as he knows only too well that with wines it is almost impossible to do this. I know many well-known experts on fine wines who could learn a great deal from Ronald Barton. This man is relatively indifferent to his surroundings. If he needs to change the wallpaper in the dining room he will always choose the same one as before. If by chance he purchases a painting, the frame must be identical with those of the portraits of his ancestors that have been hanging in the Langoa drawing room for a century and a half. It is interesting to note that Swissair serves Château Léoville Barton to its first-class passengers.

Anthony Barton is Ronald's nephew. His grandfather Bertram, better known as Uncle Berty, intended him to come to France ever since he was a child. He landed at Bordeaux in 1951, aged 21, a thoroughbred product of Cambridge, without knowing a single word of French. His wife Eva, who is Danish in origin and character, has borne him two children, the charming Lilian and the unexpected Thomas whose name follows in the tradition of the Barton family in Bordeaux, ever since the arrival of French Tom in the early eighteenth century. Anthony is in the process of becoming the lord of Léoville and Langoa Barton. The commercial house of Barton and Guestier which was bought by Seagram a few years ago, no longer has any Barton or Guestier among its personnel, but the life of the two great *crus classés* of Saint-Julien continues to overcome all obstacles, thanks to the continuing tradition guaranteed by Anthony.

The lion of Léoville Las Cases acts as an imperial guard.

The wines of Léoville Barton, like those of Langoa, are not as celebrated in France and on the rest of the Continent as they are in the Anglo-Saxon countries. This is a great shame, as those who appreciate the great classic Médoc wines could find magnificent vintages at Léoville Barton, which can compete with the best Bordeaux *crus*.

Léoville Las Cases (Château)

Commune: Saint-Julien-Beychevelle **Owner:** Société civile du Château Las Cases **Administrator:** Michel Delon **Commercial director:** Jacques Depoizier **Chef de culture:** Jean Nemetz **Maître de chai:** Michel Rolland **Surface area of vineyard:** 85 hectares (total property 147 hectares) **Average age of vines:** 30 years **Grape production:** 67% Cabernet-Sauvignon, 17% Merlot, 13% Cabernet-Franc, 3% Petit-Verdot **Production:** Approximately 300,000 bottles for Léoville Las Cases; approximately 80,000 bottles for Clos du Marquis (labelled) **Retail sales:** All major Bordeaux house.

2e *cru classé*

The Château Léoville Las Cases is sometimes called the 'Latour of Saint-Julien'. Château Latour could also be considered as the 'Léoville of Pauillac'. The small stream, the Juillac, traces the dividing line between the two large, beautiful vineyards. The estate of Léoville Las Cases is bordered by a wall with a rounded summit and the entrance is formed by a monumental gateway, with a triumphal arch worthy of the powerful tractors which pass through it. It is guarded by a stone lion on the top. The general impression is that of a mausoleum for a Roman Emperor. You half expect to see the Palace of the Governor of the Gauls during the time of Diocletian as you pass

The tower of the church of Saint-Julien can be seen rising behind Léoville Las Cases.

through the archway. However, there is no palace, nor even a cottage. The visitor is greeted only by a marvellous garden on the banks of the river. These are the vines of Léoville Las Cases which have been surveying the river flowing calmly past for three centuries.

At the end of the seventeenth century, all of Léoville was under the control of the lordship of Lamarque, which included in particular the baronies of Beychevelle and Calon. In 1707, the president of the Trésoriers de France, Jean de Moytié, divided the fief of Calon into two and gave the second section the name of Mont-Moytié. This

second half was extremely productive, since three Léoville estates were born a century later. Jean de Moytié's two daughters did not get on very well. At the death of their father the lawyer, Lacoste, had a great deal to settle. Finally it was the wife of the local Court Judge, Blaise Antoine Alexandre de Gasq, who, with the aid of her powerful husband, lord of Léoville (in Saintonge), inherited the entire estate.

The de Gasq family was distinguished during the eighteenth century for the number of magistrates in it and for its possessions on the slopes of Bordeaux and Médoc. Blaise Jean Charles Alexandre de Gasq was an estate-owner at Issan (Cantenac-Margaux)

The vat-house of Léoville Las Cases is well equipped, with a blend of the modern and the traditional.

and owner of the *cru* known today as Château Palmer. The Gasq family also enjoyed an excellent reputation in the Barsac region. When the Maréchal de Richelieu was 'exiled' to Bordeaux, he became friendly with the de Gasq family and preferred their wines to all others. After the quality of the names of Gasq and of Léoville had become well known, Blaise de Gasq, lord of Léoville, died without heirs. The estate was shared by his four nephews, Jean-Pierre d'Embleville, Jean-Joseph and Bernard d'Alozier and Jeanne, Marquise de Lascases de Beauvoir, all part of the Abadie branch of the family. It would appear that this situation continued until the Revolution. When the Marquis emigrated, however, his estate was seized and a division became inevitable. Through a complicated lottery, the quarter of the estate confiscated by the state was sold to three individuals before it was finally reunited by Hugh Barton under the name of Léoville Barton. Another quarter was inherited by Mme d'Abadie, aunt of the Marquis de Lascases, and the remaining half became the property of the brothers d'Abadie d'Alozier. I am unaware of the exact way in which this allocation was made. One of the claimants took the title of Marquis de Lascases and was the apparent owner until 1840. Then a dispute arose over the overlapping of ownership of the buildings, between a Marquis de Lascases and his sister, Baroness de Poyferré de Cères. The label of Château Léoville Poyferré was created at that time.

Forty years later a change in the division of the estate set up the two *crus* in a more logical way and this still exists today. In 1900 Gabriel de Las Cases, who had acquired the share of his elder brother, Gaston, Marquis de Las Cases, and remained in partnership with his sister, Clothilde, got himself into financial difficulties. He sold two-thirds of his share to a group of 13 Bordeaux citizens, among whom was Théophile Skavinski. (Also involved were Calvet, Peyrelongue and Tastet.) In thirty years, Skavinski managed to draw together the scattered parts of the estate and they are today the property of his grandson, Paul Delon. The collateral branch of the Las Cases family is still a minority shareholder with the families of Alozier, de Charrin and Dillon

Kavanagh du Fertag. In spite of these complicated divisions, Léoville Las Cases is still a fine production unit and is a model of a Médoc *grand cru*. The vineyard overlooks the river and is mainly situated between the Pauillac road and the river, immediately to the north of the village of Saint-Julien. Two less important parcels of land are to be found, one to the west and the other to the south of the town.

The wines of Léoville Las Cases are often masterpieces of balance between vigour and suppleness, elegance and richness, fullness and generosity. In good years, they have an extraordinary intensity of bouquet and are exceptionally full. The fruit and the sap blend into a harmony which is worthy of the greatest of the great wines. I have already said that Léoville Las Cases was sometimes called the 'Latour of Saint-Julien'. I have personal experience of the accuracy of this description. I was at a dinner with some wine enthusiasts, friends of mine. Bertrand Blanchy was host, and proved to be very concerned that we should enjoy ourselves. We had fifteen *grands crus* of the 1966 vintage to taste which were served in three sets of five glasses. We were, of course, taking part in a blind tasting, which means only our host knew the identity of the *cru*. He was in sparkling form that night and had divided a magnum into two, serving it for the second and third sets of glasses. This wine was offered in normal decanters, as were the others. This test, which is only amusing for the person who arranges it, is the worst trick that one can play on an experienced wine-taster. The relativity of each wine varies considerably according to its neighbour and when it is served during the meal. All my friends and I have often been taken in by this sort of test. On this occasion I was able to identify the same wine used for number 5 in the second service of glasses and for number 3 in the third service of glasses. (We had not been warned that an anonymous magnum had been concealed among the others.) Several times I gave it first place in each service and I identified it as a Léoville Las Cases. What a terrible mistake! It was a Latour! This was nothing to boast about. However, it is an anecdote which I like to recount. I did tell you at the beginning of this section that Latour is the 'Léoville of Pauillac'.

Michel Delon is administrator of Château Léoville Las Cases and is a gentleman farmer both efficient and discreet. He runs his vineyard and *chai* as an aristocratic and enlightened specialist without missing any opportunity for improvement. When you hear him pronounce the name of Las Cases, you are very much aware that there is some close relationship between the land and the man. It is a relationship which is as mysterious as love. The wine of Léoville Las Cases is a beautiful love child.

Léoville Poyferré (Château)

Commune: Saint-Julien-Beychevelle **Owner:** Société civile des Domaines de Saint-Julien **Director:** Didier Cuvelier **Chef de culture:** Jean-Pierre Fatin **Maître de chai:** Francis Dourthe **Surface area of vineyard:** 60 hectares (total property 100 hectares) **Average age of vines:** 30 years **Grape production:** 75% Cabernet-Sauvignon, 25% Merlot **Production:** 300,000 bottles **Local sales:** Tel (56) 59 08 30, **and by direct mail:** Ets Cuvelier & Fils, 72 rue Regnier, 33000 Bordeaux **Retail sales:** Several firms in Bordeaux

2ᵉ cru classé

The pallets and cases will soon make way for a new formal courtyard.

The Société civile des Domaines de Saint-Julien is made up of the Cuvelier family group. This family came from Haubourdin, in the *département* of Nord in 1904, when they bought the Château Le Crock at Saint-Estèphe, near the little village of Marbuzet. They were also owners of Château Camensac, a *cru classé* of Saint-Laurent. Léoville Poyferré was bought in 1921, at which time it belonged to the Lalande heirs, a family which had been powerfully placed in the Bordeaux wine trade for a century. Armand Lalande was *député* for Médoc at the end of the last century. His daughter married a Lawton. At Léoville Poyferré he had an associate called d'Erlanger. Previously this estate was made when the property of Alexandre de Gasq was divided into three (see the other Léoville). This happened when a daughter of Jean de Las Cases married Baron Jean-Marie de Poyferré from Cères, a commune on the moors 10 kilometres to the north of Mont-de-Marsan. The Poyferré family is an old, well-established family from Gascony. After Jean-Marie's death his son, who was badly advised by a Bordeaux banker, made some risky investments, in particular in the shares of the Russian railways, which led directly to his ruin. Jean de Poyferré today represents the younger branch of the family, as the senior branch has been extinct for a generation. He has returned to the country of his ancestors, where he produces one of the best possible Armagnacs, sold under the label of Domaine de Jouanda, at Arthez in Armagnac. The most junior of his wonderful brandies is at least twenty years old. What more could you want?

Let us, however, return to Saint-Julien and visit the present owner of Léoville Poyferré. He is Max Cuvelier, the head of the family who manages both the commercial activity and the wine producing. After studying as an accountant, his son Didier, who is now 30 years old, became fascinated by Poyferré and he now looks after the business. A heavy investment programme is under way. Léoville Poyferré was lagging behind the other major *crus classés* in Médoc from the point of view of equipment. Several generations of the Delon family (owners of Château Phélan-Ségur in Saint-Estèphe), had looked after the estate in rather a casual way and it seemed to have been overcome by lethargy. Quality was not very evident, and the wine had fallen from the group in which the 1855 classification had placed it. During the last twenty years I cannot recall having tasted a single vintage from them which has aroused my admiration. However, all that is in the process of changing. It seems to me that the arrival

Behind this doorway considerable improvements are now taking place.

of Didier Cuvelier will bring a welcome injection of new blood. The vat-house is in the process of being totally renovated. An ultra-modern reception area for the harvest has been installed as well as fermentation vats each with a capacity of 300 hectolitres. The *chai* for the new wine is impressive, and half the stock of casks is replaced every year. The interior of the buildings is well maintained. There is, however, room still for improvement in the yard to the left of the road, coming from Beychevelle and this is being planned. This, of course, is not essential in producing a high-quality wine, but it would help greatly in maintaining what is now known as a 'quality image'.

Generally speaking, the great *crus classés* (and many others) have made considerable progress in recent years. As far as the vineyard is concerned, Léoville Poyferré is divided into six parcels of land of different sizes. The largest is to the west of the town of Saint-Julien and extends to the Juillac, facing the estate of Pichon-Lalande. Leaving the village, in the direction of Pauillac, the main road acts as a border between Las Cases to the right and Poyferré to the left. If it were not there, you would notice a continuity between the two vineyards. The Cuvelier family also possess the former 169 estate of Château Moulin Riche, whose label is used as a second brand and distributed exclusively by the family business.

The wine-making process has been approved by Professor Peynaud, and with the help of the dynamic and intelligent Didier Cuvelier, Léoville Poyferré is in the process of regaining its original high rank. I have no doubt that in future the competition between the three Léoville wines will be very keen.

Les Ormes (Château)

cru artisan

Commune: Saint-Julien-Beychevelle **Owner:** René Durand **Surface area of vineyard:** 1.5 hectares **Average age of vines:** Approximately 30 years **Grape production:** 70% Cabernet, 25% Merlot, 5% Petit-Verdot **Production:** 6–7 *tonneaux.* **Sales:** Depending on the year, the *cru* is sold on site to the trade, sometimes in bulk. The owner plans in future to offer all his wines for sale at the château.

Harvest time at the Château Les Ormes is the opportunity for a family party to which friends are always welcomed by René Durand and his wife. Their house, which is in Beychevelle, is built of stone and bricks, and decorated in the style of the late nineteenth century. It could well be the subject of a postcard of Biarritz or Deauville. The small patch of garden is interestingly planted with wonderful cacti which add to the exotic character of the front of the house. Until last year, René Durand shared with his brother both the trade of roof tiler and the three parcels of vineyards amounting to 1½ hectares close to Talbot, Saint-Pierre and Beaucaillou. They decided on a friendly separation and René Durand, giving up his interest in the roof trade, received in exchange all of the vineyard. The 1984 harvest was his first on an independent basis. His grandfather was *maître de chai* at Château Lagrange when it was in its full splendour. The secrets of traditional wine-making are well known to his grandson.

René Durand is not averse to a bit of shooting when the season opens, and he is particularly fond of woodcock. Pacha, his six-year-old setter, could tell you many stories about woodcock. He finds them and René shoots them; Pacha then retrieves them and René carries them back to his home, where they are hung for five days before being carefully plucked but not drawn. Slices of bread are flavoured with garlic and spread with butter, and then the woodcock, covered with strips of bacon, are hung in front of the fire on a string with the bread placed below them. They turn slowly with a little help if necessary, and slowly drip their juices on to the bread. When the woodcock are cooked they are served whole with boiled potatoes – unless of course mushrooms are available. A glass of old wine is delicious with this dish. Solange Durand, whose recipe this is, has many others but I have promised not to reveal all her family secrets. She is a cousin of the Feillon brothers who themselves make an excellent wine in the Côtes de Bourg, on the other side of the estuary, under the name of Château Les Roques.

The label for Château Les Ormes is number 396 in the catalogue of the Wetterwald printing works in Bordeaux. It is an old-fashioned label, which I find very attractive. But I prefer the wine, even without the woodcock...

Marquis (Clos du) 🍷 ♟♟♟♟♟
→ *Léoville du marquis de Las Cases*

Marquis de Lalande 🍷 ♟♟♟♟♟
→ *Glana*

Moulin de la Bridane (Château) 🍷
→ *Capdelong* ♟♟♟♟♟

Moulin de la Rose (Château) ♟♟♟♟♟

Commune: Saint-Julien-Beychevelle **Owner:** Guy Delon **Consultant:** Emile Peynaud **Surface ares of vineyard:** 4 hectares **Average age of vines:** 25 years **Grape production:** 55% Cabernet-Sauvignon, 30% Merlot, 15% Cabernet-Franc and Petit-Verdot **Production:** 24,000 bottles **Local sales:** Tel (56) 59 08 45, **and by direct mail:** Château Moulin de la Rose, 33250 Saint-Julien-Beychevelle

cru bourgeois

Sunday 1 October 1978 was a lucky day for Guy Delon. On that day, Victor Franco wrote a two column article in the *Journal du Dimanche* with the charming title of 'Lilliput among the giants of Médoc'. In the article he praised the Moulin de la Rose and its owner. Victor Franco, as I know well, has a lively interest in anything to do with wine. I would even say that he is an experienced amateur wine taster. He is, however, still very much a journalist and never misses a chance to find something sensational. He started his article as follows: 'I don't know anybody smaller than Guy Delon in Saint-Julien-Beychevelle, that village of Médoc which houses eleven of the most famous *grands crus* as qualified by the classification of 1855.' The line of attack is subtle, especially when you are aware of the size of the author. (I do not know anybody in the Paris press who is smaller than Victor Franco.) I am certain, however, that

171

The Moulin de la Rose is in the heart of the village of Beychevelle.

Franco made the comparison of a certain number of bottles produced by a Saint-Julien *cru* with a certain number of enthusiastic readers. If, for example, he had written about Jean-François Fillastre and his Domaine de Jaugaret, or about Jean Cazeau and his Domaine Castaing, or even about some of the other 'small' wine-producers of Saint-Julien who can be counted on the fingers of both hands, the 3000 bottles produced each year by any one of them would not have 'softened' two columns of a major newspaper in the capital. While respecting the real talent of Victor Franco and his sense of occasion, I am nevertheless tempted to say that Guy Delon, owner of the Château Moulin de la Rose, is one of the smallest of the great owners, or the greatest of the small wine-producers in Saint-Julien. Six years ago Franco stated that there was an average production of 12,000 bottles annually whereas Guy Delon declares an average 24,000 (207 hectolitres in 1983 for 3.92 hectares, which corresponds to a yield of 52 hectolitres per hectare, a 'satisfactory' nominal yield). Having said this, Guy Delon cannot be considered a small wine-producer since he also runs, as co-owner, the Château Phélan-Ségur, a *grand cru bourgeois* of Saint-Estèphe which, with its 60 hectares of land, produces more than 200 *tonneaux* every year.

Guy Delon's father bought the Moulin de la Rose in 1961 from M. Martet. Ten years later, wishing to take things a little easier, he gave his son the management of the estate, which is divided into 25 parcels of land under 60 different land registration numbers. Since 1971, when he took over the business, Guy Delon has come through the Bordeaux wine crisis which lasted from 1973 to 1975. He drew his personal con-clusions from that period and has decided not to depend on local trade. He therefore

172

took steps to arrange the bottling of all his production and to have space for holding his stock. Things were a little difficult at first but his family connections were strong enough to create an initial direct clientele. When the article by Victor Franco appeared, Guy Delon was overwhelmed with orders and sold 15,000 bottles in six weeks. Nowadays he is well supplied with customers.

I must point out that Guy Delon has among his ancestors at least four generations of wine producers. His son, aged 15, is a pupil at the Agricultural School at Blanquefort on the borders of Médoc. This man, who is always concerned with quality, is worried about the present and the future. The French economy disturbs his sleep as he sees the purchasing power of his customers being reduced. He is particularly worried about French taxes. However, he has enough friends to be able to sell all his production without difficulty.

The vat-house is up to date and has stainless steel vats. The wine matures in oak casks which are bought second-hand from the great *crus classés*, such as Château Lafite-Rothschild. All the processes are carried out in the strictly traditional Médoc way. The wine of Moulin de la Rose is very much of the 'Saint-Julien' type. The proportion of Merlot grapes gives it an unexpected suppleness, while the larger proportion of Cabernet grapes have sufficient strength to make their tannin content felt. Victor Franco was right to mention him in his newspaper. The Château Moulin de la Rose offers excellent quality for the price.

Moulin Riche (Château)

→ *Léoville Poyferré*   *cru bourgeois supérieur exceptionnel*

Ortolan (Cru)

Commune: Saint-Julien-Beychevelle **Owner:** Mme Pierina Ortolan **Surface area of vineyard:** 200 square metres **Average age of vines:** 20 years **Grape production:** 60% Cabernet-Sauvignon, 35% Merlot, 5% Petit-Verdot **Production:** Approximately 1000 bottles **Local sales:** Tel (56) 59 22 35, **and by direct mail:** Cru Ortolan, 33250 Saint-Julien-Beychevelle

The Ortolan *cru* is a rare bird. As everyone knows, the species is in danger of becoming extinct. Ortolans were considered a delicacy in former times; famous gourmets such as Brillat-Savarin, Dodin Bouffant, Prosper Montagné and Curnonsky shed many a gastronomic tear at the thought of the succulent little bird which is now protected.

Little wine-producers of the size of Ortolan in Beychevelle should also be protected. I would adapt the comment of Victor Franco quoted in the previous section and say quite definitely that: 'I do not know anything smaller than Ortolan in Saint-Julien.' Two thousand square metres of vines are there as a witness, with a yield of about 1200 bottles in a good year.

Mme Pierina Ortolan is, as her first name indicates, of Italian origin. She came from Lorraine in 1939 and lived in the port house of Beychevelle from 1949 to 1956. Her

M. Mario Ortolan, one mechanical cultivator and 200 square metres of vines produce between them the entire Cru Ortolan.

husband was called the 'port sailor': he looked after the sailing boats of Armand Achille-Fould. The estuary held no secrets for him. He was very clever at fishing and at catching prawns and eels. Every Saturday his family went to the market at Blaye, and on Saint Catherine's day they bought piglets in order to rear them. Today Pierina Ortolan has six children and thirteen grandchildren. Her son Mario could plough the vineyard when he was 12 years old. When he was 15 he was employed to look after the vines at the Martin property but he could also work in the *chai*.

Nowadays, when all the family get together in the little house in Beychevelle, there are 26 people at table. On holidays Pierina Ortolan (better known locally as Pierrette), reminds her little world of their origins by preparing home-made ravioli. She usually starts cooking on Friday, in order to be ready for Sunday: you need some time to cook 600 ravioli. 'I cook by instinct, not be measuring,' she says, like those artists of the Quattrocento who had an innate sense of proportion. The harvest presents no problem, as all the family lend a hand. There are plenty of them and no charge is made. The grapes are picked by hand, and are then crushed with a stick in the vat and stirred twice a day. The eggs for fining are provided by their own chickens. There is no label. The wine is sent to cousins in Lorraine, Niort, Le Havre, Lyons and the Basque country simply clarified and bottled. I have promised to design a label for them showing an ortolan eating grapes. This is as good a way as any to help protect the breed.

Peymartin (Château)

→ *Gloria*

Réserve de l'Amiral

→ *Beychevelle*

Saint-Julien (Clos)

→ *Teynac*

Saint-Pierre (Château)

4ᵉ cru classé

Commune: Saint-Julien-Beychevelle **Owner:** Henri Martin **Director:** Jean-Louis Triaud **Chef de culture:** Maurice Andron **Maître de chai:** Jean-Marie Galey Berdier **Surface area of vineyard:** 15 hectares (total property 38 hectares) **Average age of vines:** 30 years **Grape production:** 70% Cabernet-Sauvignon, 25% Merlot, 5% Cabernet-Franc **Production:** 70,000 bottles **Local sales:** Tel (56) 59 08 18, **and by direct mail:** Château Saint-Pierre, 33250 Saint-Julien-Beychevelle **Retail sales:** Several firms in Bordeaux

In 1921 Colonel Kappelhoff, owner of the Château Saint-Pierre-Bontemps, which qualified as a *4ᵉ cru* in 1855, asked Alfred Martin, a cask-maker by trade and father of Henri Martin (see Château Gloria), to take over the management of the *cru*. It was not a favourable time for trading in wine and many producers of the great *crus* were losing money. In return for his work and in addition to a tenancy contract, Alfred

Château Saint-Pierre is in the process of being completely renovated.

Martin also obtained the possibility of storing all the new casks which he made every day and which, as they were only delivered just before the harvest, needed considerable storage space. Two years later, the owner resigned himself to selling his property. The Martin family bought the *chais* which held their casks but could not afford more than a few vines. The label of Château Saint-Pierre-Bontemps passed into the hands of Charles Van den Bussche, an important wine-merchant in Antwerp, while Saint-Pierre Sevaistre was bought by M. Bernheim, to be sold a few years later to the Van den

Bussche brothers. The two labels circulated either separately or together for several decades.

The history of Saint-Pierre from the origins of the *cru* to the present day is highly complicated. The estate is a result, also, of the disintegration of the barony of Beychevelle before, during and after the Revolution. There are two conflicting theories. One dates the creation of the estate to 1693, that is about thirty years after the death of Bernard de la Valette, second Duke of Epernon, and at the time Président d'Abbadie purchased Beychevelle. At that time the *cru* existed under the name of Serançan, and Féret's book *Bordeaux et ses vins* states that the Cheverry family was the owner. The other theory, which seems just as plausible, is that Saint-Pierre was extracted from the estate of Bedout, when M. Bergeron appropriated half the lands of the lordship of Lamarque and among them what was to become Ducru-Beaucaillou (see section under this name). Bedout was briefly included in the list of good Saint-Julien *crus* before it was bought by the Baron de Saint-Pierre in 1767, and then became a *4ᵉ cru classé* in 1855. In 1836 he had divided the estate between his three heirs: Colonel Bontemps-Dubarry, Mme Roullet and Mme Galoupeau. The Saint-Pierre *crus* began to appear everywhere and Mme de Bedout returned from heaven knows where to the 'Chalet Teinac' (see Château Teynac). She stayed there during the building of 'Chalet Saint-Pierre' (today the Château du Glana), carried out by the active and intelligent M. Cayx. After a century the descendants of Baron de Saint-Pierre had created so many children that the *cru* lost its stature.

I would like to digress a little here on the problem of second brands for châteaux. This is a contemporary problem and an attempt to solve it has been made by forbidding the use of the word 'château' for the second choice of wines from a *cru* even if it was classified as first. Formerly, the quality was clearly stated by the owner who sold his *cru* as a 'first wine' (or *grand vin*, as explained previously) and a 'second wine'. Nowadays the excessive proliferation of 'châteaux' has made it necessary to tighten the rules in using this description, a concern that seems justified to me. However, we still need to find a final solution. There is no general way for the consumer to differentiate between the numerous phoney 'château' labels used by what are called basic Bordeaux appellations and the carefully selected 'château' name given by the owner of a *cru classé* or a *bourgeois cru* to a respectable Médoc appellation.

The chance example of Saint-Pierre in Saint-Julien may well supply us with a guide for establishing a clear system of categories. The term 'chalet', which means exactly what it says, could possibly be used as a prefix for secondary brands. The Châteaux Saint-Pierre, Ducru-Beaucaillou, Branaire, Talbot, etc., could offer their products which could be judged to be 'declassified' (but which for the most part are of good quality) as wines of Chalet Saint-Pierre etc. Once the public is made aware of this basic information, the legal status of wines labelled in this way would replace the fantasy brands based on vague geographical or historical connections.

After Saint-Pierre was dissected, there was a blossoming of a whole range of brands such as Clos Saint-Julien, Cru de La Rose-de-France, Château La Fleur Saint-Julien, Château Saint-Louis du Bosq, Cru Saint-Marc and so on, all of which had a general air of sanctity about them. In fact two labels from a Saint-Pierre *cru classé* existed together for more than a century. Saint-Pierre-Bontemps descended directly into the possession of Colonel Bontemps-Kappelhoff, grandson of Colonel Bontemps-Dubarry. The Misses Kappelhoff, the last heiresses, used the brand of Château Bontemps-Dubarry for a limited production, while Saint-Pierre-Bontemps was bought by Van den Bussche, and subsequently used by his son-in-law Paul Castelein. Saint-Pierre-Sevaistre was created by Léon Sevaistre, a former deputy for the Eure and mayor of Elbeuf, when he bought her part of the estate from Mme de Luetkens, sister of Colonel Bontemps-Dubarry. After him his son-in-law Charles Legras remained the owner for some years. At the end of this saga it is Henry Martin who is now the sole proprietor of Château Saint-Pierre, having succeeded in bringing together the various constituent parts of the estate.

Changes in the hereditary succession of the estate made it possible for him to buy the château in 1982, after having spent the previous forty years patiently working at reuniting the vineyard. His father had bequeathed to him the *chais* that he had owned since 1921. The personal success of Henri Martin cannot be better illustrated than by his resurrection of a *cru classé*. For the first time in two hundred years Château Saint-Pierre is no longer looking for its own identity. The vineyard today has been more or

A watercolour of the architect's plan for Château Talbot.

less restored to its original size of 1855, at the heart of the Saint-Julien appellation. The château and its *chais* are situated at the entrance to the village of Beychevelle, near Château Gloria. Of course these two *crus* have the same owner, but Henri Martin is emphasizing the difference between them more and more so that each shall have its own individuality. Secondary labels are used for additional brands (see Château Gloria). The wine of Saint-Pierre does not lack breeding. It is vigorous, rich and high in tannin, which makes it very suitable for keeping. The bouquet is very typical of Saint-Julien. The wine also possesses the finesse and the subtlety of its owner, Henri Martin. A slightly longer period of maturing in casks would sometimes be desirable. However, having said this, Saint-Pierre and Henri Martin are a winning team.

Talbot (Château)

Commune: Saint-Julien-Beychevelle **Owner:** Jean Cordier **Director:** Jean Cordier **Consultant:** Georges Pauli, director of Domaines Cordier **Manager:** Henri Pujoz **Chef de culture:** Jean-Marie Bouin **Maître de chai:** Serge Potier **Surface area of vineyard:** 100 hectares (total property 160 hectares) **Average age of vines:** 35 years **Grape production:** 70% Cabernet-Sauvignon, 20% Merlot, 5% Cabernet-Franc, 5% Petit-Verdot **Production:** 450,000 bottles **Retail sales:** Ets Cordier, quai de Paludate, 33000 Bordeaux

4ᵉ cru classé

Mlle Nancy Cordier.   *An old label of Château Talbot.*

On the label of Château Talbot there is the following inscription: 'Formerly the estate of Connétable Talbot, Governor of the Province of Guyenne, 1400–1453'. This is rather a fanciful way of writing history, since General Talbot, Earl of Shrewsbury, was never a landowner in Médoc. However, he felt very much at home there, like many an occupying military force. We would also express doubts as to the existence of any vineyard worthy of this description at the beginning of this century in the region of Saint-Julien de Rinhac. The presumed origin of the Château Talbot name belongs in the realms of legend. Many place-names in Guyenne and Gascony are similar to the name Talbot, which the geographer Belleyme at the end of the eighteenth century spelt as Talabot. It could also be a family name of Gascon origin, thus creating a phonetic confusion with the name of Henry IV's chief general. However, it is known that Château Talbot belonged for two centuries to the Marquis d'Aux, a very ancient family from Armagnac.

The family of the Marquis d'Aux have also left their mark on the label of the Château Patache d'Aux at Bégadan, an ancient coaching station in the Bas-Médoc. There was also a M. Delage at Talbot towards the end of the seventeenth century. It would be easy to conclude that Château Talbot was formerly a museum for vintage cars ...

With its hundred hectares of vines in the heart of the Saint-Julien appellation, Talbot is a dream property brought to life by the château, the *chais*, the vat-house, the other adjacent buildings and the park. The very large parcels of land benefit from their situation on gentle slopes, consisting of the oldest alluvial soil. Their sub-stratum is clay limestone, mixed with sandstone. The land slopes towards the river and a network of streams and springs ensures perfect drainage, essential for the frugal requirements of the vine. Médoc tradition maintains that the vine must 'face the river'. This means that the irrigation of the site must, of course, lead directly to the river. Experience has shown that irrigation flowing in a westerly direction is less favourable for producing *grand cru* wines. Talbot is on the watershed of the stony slopes of Saint-Julien and at 22 metres it is one of the highest vineyards in the appellation. The visitor will be impressed by the impeccable appearance of the vineyard and of the wine-making

Like its 'elder brother' Gruaud-Larose, Talbot is impeccably maintained.

equipment. As an experiment Georges Cordier arranged in the thirties to have a few specimens of Sauvignon and Sémillon grapes planted to make his own personal white wine. The result was so successful that a new label was created called Le Caillou Blanc du Château Talbot. It is similar to the Pavillon Blanc of Château Margaux.

Désiré Cordier bought Talbot in 1918, one year after his purchase of Gruaud-Larose. He presented it to his son, Georges. Château Talbot, rather than Gruaud-Larose, became the family residence of the Cordiers. Today it is the country retreat of Jean Cordier when he is in Bordeaux. I believe that secretly he is deeply attached to Talbot and that he feels more at ease there than in other places where he is involved with his multiple business interests. I once happened to sit opposite him for luncheon in the dining room of the château, which is decorated in a curious but successful blend of the styles of Louis XVI and Louis-Philippe. He was not at all the same man whom   181

I might have met at an air terminal or at a grand restaurant in a capital city, or even behind a massive desk in the offices of the company that carries his name. Désiré Cordier had been extremely successful in business, both in wines and commerce, to the consternation of the local aristocracy, at whom he liked to thumb his nose. He was fascinated by politics, but he rose no higher than being mayor of Saint-Julien. He was a tough character who built up a wine empire and a complicated web of business contacts. He lost a son at the end of the First World War and his youngest in 1928. Georges was the last of his generation bearing the name and in 1938 when he died, he left his son Jean, aged 14, at the head of this empire. Having taken on this responsibility very early in life, Jean Cordier soon learnt the basics of business philosophy. He has a complicated character, both jovial and reserved, indifferent and yet sentimental, reliable and whimsical; it is difficult to know him well.

Like Gruaud-Larose, Château Talbot has a superb collection of old vintages, not available commercially, which Jean Cordier delights in offering to his personal guests. Talbot is subtler than Gruaud, which means that it matures more rapidly in bottle, but does not have such a long life. The identity of each of the two *crus* is kept completely intact, even if you cannot fail to notice a '*style Cordier*' behind the two labels. It is a reliable style, constant from one year to another, and very rarely disappointing.

Terroir de la Cabane: a photograph from the Nomard family album.

Terrey-Gros-Cailloux (Château)

Commune: Saint-Julien-Beychevelle **Owner:** SDF Fort-Praderes **Surface area of vineyard:** Approximately 15 hectares **Average age of vines:** Approximately 15 years **Grape production:** 65% Cabernet-Sauvignon, 30% Merlot, 5% Petit-Verdot **Production:** Approximately 50 hectolitres per hectare **Local sales and direct mail:** Approximately one-third of each harvest **Retail sales:** Approximately two-thirds of each harvest

cru artisan

In the early fifties the Château Terrey-Gros-Cailloux was a *cru artisan* of Beychevelle and declared a production of 20 *tonneaux* each year. In the 1982 edition of *Bordeaux et ses vins* by Féret, a production of 80 *tonneaux* was declared with a note to the effect that the estate produced a wine of great merit. Present production is in fact about 100 *tonneaux*. This is a good *bourgeois cru*, but it is not noble. It could perhaps be described as an industrial craftsman.

Terroir de la Cabane

Commune: Saint-Julien-Beychevelle **Owner:** Francis Nomard **Surface area of vineyard:** 390 square metres **Average age of vines:** 50 years **Grape production:** 1/3 Cabernet, 2/3 Merlot **Production:** 20 hectolitres maximum, of which four are on sale at the château and the balance sold in bulk to the trade **Local sales:** Tel (56) 59 20 96, **and by direct mail:** Château Gloria, Le Gloria à Beychevelle, 33250 Saint-Julien-Beychevelle **Retail sales:** As a generic wine

cru artisan

Francis Nomard is a part-time wine producer who should, however, be treated seriously. The 390 square metres which he inherited from his parents lie on the central plateau of Saint-Julien near the vineyards of Talbot, Barton and Poyferré. Some of the plants are more than 80 years old. They produce very little wine but of the best quality, and they are part of the family tradition. Francis's grandmother produced her wine with the help of a donkey, which also did the ploughing and drew the carts, including the one which went to meet the family guests who arrived by train at the Saint-Laurent station. One day, while a very happy group was returning after a good meal, things got so lively that the shafts of the cart snapped off and the journey had to be continued on foot. Among the neighbours and friends of the Nomard family was M. Verdier, a cobbler from rue d'Ornano in Bordeaux, who lived near Jean Merkès, the father of the famous light opera singer, Marcel Merkès. Verdier owned 1500 vines at Saint-Julien. Harvest time was never a sad occasion!

After the harvest Francis Nomard likes to shoot a few thrushes, which are greatly enjoyed, but he never shoots more than the exact number required to make a brochette for each guest. In winter he is very keen on shooting woodcock. He hunts with René Durand. The mantelpiece in the family living room has everything needed for cooking woodcock. One evening, I recall, at a family dinner there were five woodcock roasting in front of the fire. How good they were with a glass of old wine! On another occasion

Francis and Jeannine Nomard collected 70 kilos of mushrooms. They did not know exactly what to do with them all ... As you see, the Nomard family is typical of Médoc. Francis's parents had lived at Gruaud-Larose where his father was a master wine-producer. His wife, Jeannine, who comes from Cussac, says her first memories are of Léoville Las Cases.

The Cabane estate produces a good, robust wine, velvety in texture and with a perfume of violets and almonds. A very small part of their modest production is bottled at the estate. About four to six casks are sold to the trade, as a generic wine. This is a pity. The wine of Francis Nomard should not remain anonymous.

Teynac (Château)

cru artisan supérieur

Commune: Saint-Julien-Beychevelle **Owner:** Pierre Gauthier **Surface area of vineyard:** 5.5 hectares (total property 6.5 hectares) **Average age of vines:** 30 years **Grape production:** 70% Cabernet, 25% Merlot, 5% Petit-Verdot **Production:** 25,000 bottles **Direct mail:** Savour-Club à Lancié, 69220 Belleville

The present Château Teynac is at the end of the main street in Beychevelle, before the three bends at the exit from the town in the direction of Gruaud-Larose and Lagrange. Formerly it was called the Château Saint-Pierre Sevaistre. It is also known as 'Chalet Teynac' (see Saint-Pierre). This property, which now belongs to Pierre Gauthier, was bought two generations ago, when 2 hectares were purchased from M. Legras, son-in-law of Léon Sevaistre. The vineyard was called Le Clos. The label Clos Saint-Julien existed until 1955 when the name was changed to Château Teynac in order to conform with regulations. Pierre's paternal grandfather was *maître de chai* to Léon Sevaistre for the whole of his life. His maternal grandfather was similarly employed being manager at Branaire for fifty years – surely a record! At the beginning of his career, Pierre's father, Charles, was employed at the Château Caronne-Sainte-Gemme in Saint-Laurent. During a period of leave in the First World War, he returned to get married and his son, Pierre, was born in 1918 in celebration of the armistice. Charles Gauthier subsequently started a wholesale and retail wine-business in Beychevelle. He bought various parcels of land, and by arranging several exchanges became owner of the Teynac buildings. Pierre Gauthier completed the work and, having inherited in 1976, now finds himself the owner of a small, attractive production unit, impeccably maintained, which includes about ten tiny vineyards scattered throughout the best areas of Saint-Julien.

If you produce wine you must look after the plants and the land throughout the year. Pierre Gauthier does just this, and will spare no effort to ensure the high quality of his wine. He lives in a smart house, built in the directoire style in the nineteenth century, with an immaculate garden which acts as a flowery oasis calm in the middle of Beychevelle. The 'Chalet Teynac' is a little further off. Pierre Gauthier, on the recommendation of Henri Martin, was taken on by Alexis Lichine in 1958 as a purchasing manager. He stayed there for seventeen years, until January 1975 when all the

personnel of the company were given notice. This stroke of fate, which could have been

First called Saint-Pierre-Sevaistre then Clos Saint-Julien, this building is now known as Chalet Teynac.

his downfall, was in fact a stroke of luck for him. Pierre Gauthier, at the age of 56, set off for pastures new by becoming the buyer for the Savour-Club.

Founded by Robert Descamps and Patrick Coppinger, the Savour-Club is one of the largest direct mail companies selling wine in France. It has magnificent offices at Lancié in the *département* of Rhône, near Romanèche-Thorins. The business has 150,000 clients throughout the country. The two founders were previously business consultants. Making use of their own experience they devised a skilful marketing policy, and their 'club' flourished. They have stringent standards of quality and, with sound financial management arranged by Descamps and good public relations by Coppinger, the Savour-Club has been a great success. Pierre Gauthier plunged in head-first and found himself completely at home. From his days with Lichine he knew the management of the Savour-Club and had introduced their clients to Bordeaux wines. He soon became an integral part of the organization and today controls all the purchases of Bordeaux wines for the club.

This man exudes friendliness and restlessness. He is always keen to do and say good things, and would never deceive anybody, including himself. He is punctilious about this, and when he was buyer for Lichine he would never recommend the purchase of his own wine. Feeling the weight of responsibility to himself and to Médoc tradition, he would find it difficult to negotiate personally on prices, terms and conditions for wines he had produced himself. This was his loss, as the merchants and shippers of Bordeaux liked his excellent wines and would say 'Gauthier would have no difficulty in selling his wine to himself!' Nowadays this problem has been solved in a satisfactory way and the Savour-Club takes almost all the vintages of Château Teynac. From a sense of friendship, Pierre Gauthier has kept two personal clients, one in Switzerland and the other in England, who buy from him about 3 *tonneaux* every year. 185

A cask being rinsed at Château Teynac.

The wine of Château Teynac is traditional. Its character is rather firm and hard, robust and with a good tannin content. It is matured for a year in vats and for a further year in casks in successive rotation. It is a wine for keeping, and develops to a wonderful extent after three years in bottle.

The Savour-Club offers Château Teynac wines to its members with this recommendation. It is a good way of getting it known and appreciated. I respect the qualities of Pierre Gauthier as well as the quality of his wine.

Appendix

List of owners

Picture acknowledgements
Bibliothèque Nationale, Paris: 47
Burdin, Bordeaux: 118
Douglas Metzler, Paris: 110

All the remaining pictures by
Luc Joubert, Paris, and Claude Lada.